ENDPAPER
Medical personnel at a MASH unit—an acronym for Mobile Army Surgical Hospital—spring into action on the arrival of two Bell H-13 helicopters bearing wounded soldiers from the front during the height of the Korean War. This original oil painting, based on photographs of MASH units in Korea, was created especially for *The Helicopters* by the distinguished British aviation artist John Young.

THE HELICOPTERS

Other Publications:

FIX IT YOURSELF
FITNESS, HEALTH AND NUTRITION
SUCCESSFUL PARENTING
HEALTHY HOME COOKING
UNDERSTANDING COMPUTERS
LIBRARY OF NATIONS
THE ENCHANTED WORLD
THE KODAK LIBRARY OF CREATIVE PHOTOGRAPHY
GREAT MEALS IN MINUTES
THE CIVIL WAR
PLANET EARTH
COLLECTOR'S LIBRARY OF THE CIVIL WAR
THE GOOD COOK
WORLD WAR II
HOME REPAIR AND IMPROVEMENT
THE OLD WEST

For information on and a full description of any of the
Time-Life Books series listed above, please write:

Reader Information
Time-Life Books
541 North Fairbanks Court
Chicago, Illinois 60611

*This volume is one of a series that traces the adventure and
science of aviation, from the earliest manned balloon ascension
through the era of jet flight.*

THE HELICOPTERS

by Warren R. Young

AND THE EDITORS OF TIME-LIFE BOOKS

TIME-LIFE BOOKS, ALEXANDRIA, VIRGINIA

THE AUTHOR

Warren R. Young is a former science editor of *Life* whose involvement in aviation dates back to his first solo flight in a Piper Cub during the 1940s. The author of many articles on aeronautical topics, he is a recipient of the Aviation and Space Writers Association Strebig Award and the Sherman Fairchild International Air Safety Writing Award.

THE CONSULTANTS

John F. Guilmartin Jr., the principal consultant, is a lieutenant colonel in the United States Air Force and editor of its professional journal, the *Air University Review.* He served as a helicopter instructor pilot and flight examiner in Southeast Asia, where he specialized in long-range rescue operations.

Harvey Lippincott, whose articles appear frequently in the *Journal of the American Aviation Historical Society,* is the historian and archivist of the United Technologies Corporation, where he is the curator of the personal papers and letters of helicopter pioneer Igor Sikorsky.

© 1982 Time-Life Books Inc. All rights reserved.
No part of this book may be reproduced in any form or by any electronic or mechanical means, including information storage and retrieval devices or systems, without prior written permission from the publisher, except that brief passages may be quoted for reviews.
Third printing. Revised 1987. Printed in U.S.A.
Published simultaneously in Canada.
School and library distribution by Silver Burdett Company, Morristown, New Jersey.

TIME-LIFE is a trademark of Time Incorporated U.S.A.

Library of Congress Cataloguing in Publication Data
Young, Warren R.
   The helicopters.
   (The Epic of flight)
   Bibliography: p.
   Includes index.
   1. Helicopters. I. Time-Life Books. II. Title. III. Series.
TL716.Y65   1982   629.133'352   82-10740
ISBN 0-8094-3350-8
ISBN 0-8094-3351-6 (lib. bdg.)

CONTENTS

"The way to fly is to go straight up"

On September 28, 1912, an inventive Danish engineer named Jacob C. H. Ellehammer unveiled a curious rotary-winged flying machine before a distinguished group of observers gathered on a field near Copenhagen. Among those present was His Royal Highness Prince Axel. After witnessing a demonstration of the craft, the Prince issued an official statement confirming that Ellehammer's "screw plane" had indeed "risen by its own power" into the air, thereby certifying its brief hop *(right)* as one of the earliest successful helicopter flights on record.

Nearly a quarter century more would pass before the experiments of men like Ellehammer resulted in the first practical helicopters. And during most of that time, the efforts of those who pursued the elusive goal of vertical flight would meet with the same skepticism and indifference that greeted the early champions of the airplane. Yet a small band of dedicated visionaries—notably Louis Breguet and Etienne Oehmichen of France, the Spanish marquis Raul Pateras Pescara, Wilhelm Zurovec of Austria-Hungary, Emile and Henry Berliner in the United States, and the great Russian émigré Igor Sikorsky—persisted in their belief that such machines might eventually match, if not surpass, the potential of fixed-wing aircraft. "The way to fly," Berliner once confidently predicted to a friend, "is to go straight up."

In the early years of the century, however, such confidence required unusual foresight. The ancestors of the modern helicopter were awkward contraptions plagued by balky, unreliable engines and imperfect control systems that made them hideously unstable in flight. Each of the machines pictured here and on the following pages managed to get off the ground, but only barely: Most of their flights were measured in inches of altitude. Even the best of these, the Zurovec PKZ2, never rose higher than 164 feet and could stay aloft only an hour. But their limited successes at least demonstrated that vertical flight was possible, thus paving the way for machines that would amply prove their worth in both peace and war.

Piloted by an assistant, Jacob Ellehammer's helicopter briefly lifts off the ground as its builder stands alongside to switch off the ignition. A prolific inventor, Ellehammer also designed X-ray equipment and the first fixed-wing airplane to fly in Scandinavia.

Tethered to the ground by cables, the Zurovec PKZ2 rises during an unmanned test hop near Budapest in 1918. Designed as a spy in the sky for the Austro-Hungarian air service, it was powered by three 100-hp engines and could be fitted with an observer's cockpit above the rotors. The machine was wrecked a few months later on a military demonstration flight.

Etienne Oehmichen, precariously perched aboard his balloon-assisted vertical-flight machine, hovers above the French countryside during a 1921 test flight. Oehmichen claimed that the hydrogen-filled bag merely helped stabilize the craft. A few years later, he built a helicopter that did not need the assistance of a balloon and that set an international distance record of 1,181 feet.

Henry Berliner's helicopter clears the ground at College Park, Maryland, in 1922. A contemporary description of the craft indicated that it could rise to a height of 20 feet and fly forward but noted that "the machine is not yet perfected to the extent of landing from any height with the degree of safety that is required."

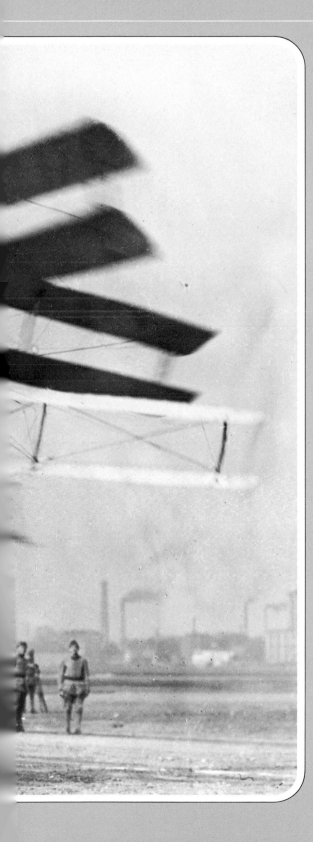

Piloted by its inventor, Raul Pateras Pescara's 16-bladed helicopter lifts off during a 1923 demonstration flight near Paris. Powered by a 180-hp engine, it incorporated an early attempt to achieve stability and control by varying the pitch, or angle, of the rotor blades. It later set a world cross-country distance record of almost half a mile.

1

Turning fantasy into reality

It began as a toy and for centuries was nothing more than that—a funny little thing that when spun between the palms of the hand or by a stem-wound string would climb into the air on whirling wings. But from this simple toy came the most wondrous of flying machines, the helicopter, an aircraft rivaling the flying carpet in its ability to go straight up or straight down, fly forward, backward or sideways, turn completely around or hover motionless in one spot.

The possibilities of vertical flight had been contemplated down through the ages. Nature had shown the first aeronautical dreamers that there might be four ways to travel into the sky: to fly like a bird, to glide like a drifting leaf, to float like a bubble or to flutter on revolving blades much like those of a maple seed. The ornithopter, a machine with flapping wings, had turned out to be an aerodynamic dead end, but by the time of the Wright brothers the drifting leaf idea had been transformed into the kite, the glider and finally the powered airplane; lighter-than-air balloons were almost commonplace, and the enormous airships of Count Ferdinand von Zeppelin would soon be known throughout the world. But the vertically lifting helicopter, whose principles were embodied in the maple seed, in hovering hummingbirds, in some insects and in an amusing toy, remained a tantalizing dream.

Numerous aeronautical theorists and experimenters had pursued that dream. Leonardo da Vinci put his superlatively inventive mind to helicopter design—and so, more than three centuries later, did Thomas Edison. Yet enormous problems had to be solved before fantasy would become reality. Large, multiengined airplanes would be spanning the globe before the first rickety helicopter would fly successfully, and years would pass before a true helicopter—one that could not only fly but be fully controlled—would at last take to the air. And then in a sudden flurry of genius, building on the pioneering work of men like Louis Breguet of France and the Russian-born Igor Sikorsky, aeronautical engineers throughout the world would transform the helicopter into a versatile machine suited to war or peace, capable of performing tasks on land, sea and air beyond the reach of other vehicles.

On the battlefield, the craft would evacuate wounded soldiers as well as deliver withering firepower against the enemy. In civil-

A 100-foot-long helicopter sails the skies in an illustration from Jules Verne's 1886 novel The Clipper of the Clouds. The airborne clipper was kept aloft by 74 electric-powered rotors and driven horizontally by enormous propellers at the bow and stern. Springs on the bottom of the hull cushioned the impact of landing.

17

ian roles, the helicopter would find hundreds of different uses: as a flying crane, hauling objects from one site to another; as a gigantic fan, drying fruit in orchards where nighttime damp might lead to rot; as an aerial fire engine, carrying water and chemicals to a raging forest fire; as a traffic monitor; as a taxicab for executives in crowded cities; as an angel of mercy, lifting passengers from storm-battered ships and plucking stranded occupants from the roofs and windows of blazing skyscrapers.

It is not known which subtle natural clue first attracted man to the notion of vertical and hovering flight. But it is known that the principle was first demonstrated in a toy. The ancient Chinese developed one they called a bamboo dragonfly, consisting of angled blades or feathers sticking out from a central bamboo stem. By the early 14th Century, toy helicopters were popular in Europe—they were probably modeled after mementos brought from Asia by travelers or by captured Tartars taken to Italy to be slaves.

Except for Leonardo da Vinci's design for a revolving wing shaped like a screw *(opposite),* the notion that the helicopter could be more than a crude toy did not gain much impetus until 1768, when the French mathematician J. P. Paucton proposed that the classic Archimedean screw—designed for lifting water—could be used for human flight. Sixteen years later another Frenchman, the naturalist Launoy, went far beyond such theorizing when he teamed up with an artisan named Bienvenu to fashion the most significant helicopter device since the first Chinese flying toy.

This simple yet clever mechanism resembled a bowspring. It consisted of a thin vertical shaft inserted through a spring steel bow, with the bowstring attached to the top of the shaft. At either end of the shaft were propellers made out of silk, their firm blades set at opposite angles to each other so that they would spin in opposite directions and generate lift. Turning the shaft wound the string, flexing the bow. When the shaft was released, the bow sprang back to shape, the string unwound and the miniature helicopter shot upward on its contrarotating propellers.

Launoy and Bienvenu demonstrated their ingenious apparatus at a gathering of the French Academy of Sciences on April 28, 1784; the device rose briskly until it hit the ceiling of the meeting room and fell to the floor. Neither the inventors nor the assembled savants realized it at the time, but the fluttering little model had overcome two fundamental barriers to helicopter development: It had a self-contained power source, and its contrarotating propellers eliminated the problem of torque, the force that would have driven a single-propeller model in a direction opposite to that of the turning shaft, preventing the craft from rising.

Cheered by the performance of their model, the two Frenchmen speculated about building a full-scale craft and going up in it them-

The first known depiction of a powered aircraft of any kind, this illustration in an early-14th Century Flemish manuscript shows a child winding up a string-pull helicopter. The everlastingly popular plaything embodies principles on which all modern helicopters operate.

Surrounded by the inventor's arcane mirror writing, a sketch of Leonardo da Vinci's model helicopter appears in one of his notebooks from the 1480s. A continuous spiral plane gave the device lift; power came from a simple clockwork mechanism. If the model was successful, as Leonardo's notes imply, it was the earliest aircraft to fly with a self-contained power source.

selves. But they soon recognized that they lacked a suitable power source and put aside any plans to rise into the heavens by means of a giant bowspring.

Launoy and Bienvenu's work might have been forgotten had it not been for an Englishman, Sir George Cayley, who, when he was 19, was inspired by a toy helicopter to devote his thoughts to heavier-than-air flight. He was destined during his long life to be the first to put the study of aeronautics on an orderly basis and would be responsible for a number of important inventions, among them the world's first flyable manned glider. But to convince others of the possibilities of heavier-than-air flight, he published, in 1809, instructions for building—"at the expense of ten minutes' labour"—a craft that resembled Launoy and Bienvenu's device but for a couple of minor differences: The propellers, or rotors, were made of feathers instead of silk, and they had four blades each rather than two. The tiny helicopter received much publicity and served, as Cayley hoped, to inspire experimentation.

Among those who were drawn to the study of vertical flight was another Englishman, one W. H. Phillips. In 1842, he built and flew a model helicopter that was powered by steam produced by the combustion of charcoal, saltpeter and gypsum. The rotor blades spun when steam was expelled from nozzles at their tips. Unfortunately for Phillips, his contrivance was uncontrollable; when he launched it for the first—and only—time, it rose quickly into the air, zoomed across two farm fields and then disappeared. After a lengthy search, Phillips reported, he "found the machine minus the wings, which had been torn off from contact with the ground." Phillips did not try again.

Cayley himself, in the meantime, seemed to have lost interest in vertical flight. While he believed that a full-sized, manned helicopter might readily be built, he dismissed the prospect: He had already deduced that a powered glider would be capable of far faster horizontal travel than a helicopter, and he spent most of his energies pursuing that approach. Nevertheless, in 1853, the year he turned 80, Cayley submitted to a French journal some drawings of yet another helicopter design. It featured a single rotor with three tin blades and a wooden launching base that was carved to fit the hand. Power was supplied by a string wound around the shaft, and a flying model of the contraption soared to the impressive height of 90 feet. What was new here, of course, was the metal rotor, which anticipated the helicopter rotors of today. Before Cayley could conduct further experiments with his model, he died, and it remained for others to pursue the possibility of vertical flight.

In the 1860s, the focus of rotary-wing theorizing and modelmaking moved from England back to France, where the Viscount Gustave de Ponton d'Amécourt built and exhibited various tiny helicopters, including a clockwork-powered model that ascended into the air, successfully remained aloft until its spring ran down, then lowered itself safely with a parachute. In 1863 he also built a steam helicopter that was two feet tall and beautifully constructed with an aluminum boiler and frame, bronze steam cylinders and two piston-driven rotors. Alas, the device could not produce enough steam pressure to hoist its own six-pound weight plus its load of water and fuel. But d'Amécourt remained a believer in the future of rotary-winged flight, and put together the Greek words *heliko* and *pteron,* meaning "spiral" and "wing," to coin an enduring name for his contrivances: He called them *hélicoptères.*

The mid-19th Century was a time of quickening technological change, and the world was being transformed by such innovations as the first oil wells, practical sewing machines, undersea telegraph cables, electricity, swift steamships and rudimentary internal combustion engines. New ideas for helicopters kept coming, too, and the rising aeronautical genius of this era was another Frenchman, Alphonse Pénaud, whose crippling hip ailment had prevented him from joining his father, an admiral, in a naval career. Pénaud had been encouraged to take up the study of flight by an aviation enthusiast named Gabriel de La Landelle.

By the time he was 20, in 1870, Pénaud had found a way to improve greatly the efficiency of the toy helicopters invented by Launoy and Bienvenu and refined by Cayley. He devised the twisted rubber-band "motor," which immediately became the classic system for powering model aircraft of all types. This innovation allowed him to build models

Sketches by British aeronautical pioneer Sir George Cayley depict the flying toy he designed in 1853 whose angled blades clearly anticipated the modern helicopter rotor. Such devices were known as Chinese tops in Cayley's day.

that were cheap, effective and not readily broken. Weighing only a fraction of an ounce, Pénaud's helicopters were marvels of delicate precision, with tiny parts of aluminum—a rare and expensive metal at the time—and paper rotor blades coated with gold to improve their flying qualities. The dainty models would sometimes dart to an altitude of 50 feet, then fall, flashing, to earth; on other occasions, they would rise only half as high but hover there for as long as 26 seconds, longer than any other toy helicopter of the day, sustained by the power of their rubber-band motors.

Pénaud's ingenious models inspired many variations, large and small, as other inventors struggled to develop a workable helicopter. But they all lacked a suitable engine, a lightweight power source that was strong enough to lift a man-carrying machine into the air. So frustrating were the failures—and so galling was the ridicule—that Alphonse Pénaud committed suicide at the age of 30. Yet if the helicopter had lost one of its most zealous advocates, it soon gained another partisan in Thomas Alva Edison.

Gabriel de La Landelle's 1863 "Steam Air Liner" uses eight lifting rotors on two masts, each topped with an umbrella parachute. It also has two large wings, a rear propeller and a hanging gondola for passengers.

A tongue-in-cheek view of the 20th Century shows gentlefolk strolling through the air with rotors strapped to their backs.

Farfetched flights of fancy

By the second half of the 19th Century, widely celebrated balloon ascents and attempts at heavier-than-air flight had fired the public imagination with dreams of powered aircraft. Bizarre schemes for flying machines appeared in a variety of publications. Most of the designs were for ornithopters that flapped like birds and offered no hope of practicability, but some employed airscrews, and some of those used screws to provide lift.

The examples of imaginary helicopters shown on these pages range from the purely whimsical to the earnest propaganda of enthusiasts like Gabriel de La Landelle *(left)* and the eminent photographer Nadar *(below, right)*. The craft in Nadar's 1864 drawing seem to have been based on the inventions of his colleague in the French Société d'Aviation, Gustave de Ponton d'Amécourt, but d'Amécourt's tiny clockwork toys never reached anything like the altitude in the drawing, and his steam-powered model never left the ground.

While most of these craft were never built, much less flown, Landelle's fantasy appears, at least, to have been influential: It is probably the direct antecedent of the vertical-flight machine in Jules Verne's *Clipper of the Clouds (page 16),* which inspired a new generation of helicopter enthusiasts, among them the man who ultimately became the world's foremost helicopter designer, Igor Sikorsky.

Twin rotors lift an "aerial carriage" in this 1874 engraving. The plume of exhaust suggests that steam is the power source, but there are no evident means of control.

The aeronaut pedals his way through the air on this 1877 contraption; both the lifting rotor and the rear propeller are powered by his legs. Handlebars control the rudder.

The helicopters in Nadar's illustration feature multiple coaxial rotors and umbrella parachutes. One is steam-powered; the other two may have tiny clockwork motors.

In the early 1880s, fresh from his triumphs with the phonograph and the electric light bulb, the prolific American inventor set himself the task of developing what he called a "helicoptal aeroplane." The first experiments at his Menlo Park, New Jersey, laboratory were designed to perfect the concept of rotor blades as lifting devices. And at the time, before the development of usable internal combustion engines, it was logical for Edison to assume that electricity would power the way into the sky. Edison could have predicted from the start that the weight of batteries would make a battery-powered helicopter or airplane as impractical as one trailing a wire to draw current from a ground-based power plant. Nevertheless, an electric motor was still the ideal energy source for his initial test-stand trials of airscrews. But when he began his experiments, rigging the stand with various kinds of propellers, the results were decidedly discouraging. The most lift he could achieve from any of his rotors amounted to scarcely five pounds of upward thrust.

Edison did not give up. Try, try again was his style. Besides, he had a wealthy financial backer: James Gordon Bennett, the famed editor of the *New York Herald,* had offered to foot the bill to get Edison started on aeronautical research, knowing that anything he came up with—particularly a wild idea—would make a good story.

Bennett, who in 1869 had dispatched Henry Stanley to Africa to find the long-lost missionary David Livingstone, had much in common with Edison. Both men were eccentric, irascible, cocksure and possessed of a genius for getting publicity. And they shared an uncanny knack for following inspired hunches. Bennett greatly admired the inventor, and he hoped to sponsor the first piloted, powered aircraft—if the Wizard of Menlo Park could come through again.

After his initial disappointments, Edison decided to take a radical approach. "What was needed was a very powerful engine for its weight," he wrote. "So I conceived of an engine employing guncotton. I took a lot of tickertape, turned it into guncotton, and got up an engine with an arrangement whereby I could feed this guncotton strip into the cylinder and explode it inside electrically. The feed took place between two copper rolls. The copper kept the temperature down as the strip was in contact with the feed rolls. It worked pretty well; but one machine roll didn't take it and the flame went through and exploded the whole roll and kicked up such an explosion that I abandoned it."

One of his men was badly burned, and Edison himself had some of his hair singed. "It was like playing with dynamite," he said, but he remained convinced that "the solution to aerial navigation was only a matter of experiment. I reported to Mr. Bennett that when an engine could be made that would weigh only three or four pounds to the horsepower, the problems of the air would be solved."

Edison quietly dropped his active research into vertical flight. Yet he never lost his conviction that the helicopter was the ultimate vehicle for the sky. "Whatever progress the aeroplane might make," he insisted years later, "the helicopter will come to be taken up by the advanced students of aeronautics."

With Edison's departure from helicopter research, there would be little significant progress in the field for nearly a generation—although a number of people tried their hands at designing contrivances for vertical flight. Indeed, one of the most important contributions to helicopter design during this period may well have been a novel written by Jules Verne. First published in French in 1886, the work appeared in English the following year as *The Clipper of the Clouds* and featured a huge, airgoing vessel with 37 masts carrying suspensory airscrews instead of sails. Verne's fantastic clipper, named the *Albatross,* incorporated a hull built of treated paper too hard for a Bowie knife to scratch; it also boasted what Verne called "piles and accumulators" (which used secret acids and positive and negative plates to produce electricity for power), lightweight engine parts and screws made of gelatinized fiber, and under the hull "a system of flexible springs to ease off the concussion when it became advisable to land." With one propeller on the bow and one on the stern for forward and reverse movement, the imaginary craft could sail around the world in a mere eight days.

Among the many readers to be enchanted and inspired by Verne's artful helicopter fantasy was Louis Charles Breguet, whose great-great-grandfather had founded the famous family concern of Maison Breguet, makers of fine watches, scientific instruments and electrical equipment. Breguet had been born on December 31, 1879; his father died before Louis was three years old, and the boy was taken under the wing of Charles Richet, a family associate and renowned scientist, who encouraged his young charge's avid interest in aviation. While at school Breguet filled his notebooks with sketches of aircraft he hoped to build.

After graduation, Breguet faithfully took up his duties with the family enterprise. By 1905, he was chief engineer in charge of "motor services" at the Maison Breguet factory at Douai and had designed and built the electric motors for two submarines. But his success meant that he had less time to indulge his passion for aviation—a passion that had recently been intensified by the writings of Colonel Charles Renard, who argued that vertical-lift machines should be taken as seriously as airplanes.

Breguet's interests in aeronautics had also been piqued by news of the Wright brothers' first flight at Kitty Hawk in 1903. But if he was disappointed that the airplane had beaten the helicopter into the air, he was undismayed, for he believed that the helicopter might yet overtake the fledgling airplane.

Nevertheless, Breguet did not rush headlong into the race. Instead, he began with a systematic study of the various elements of his planned

In the sequence at left, Connecticut inventor John Newton Williams demonstrates the launch, flight and retrieval of the spring-powered model helicopter he built in 1905. Williams constructed a full-sized version of the device in 1908; it lifted him a few inches off the ground during tests but proved incapable of sustained flight.

machines. During 1905, as a private side project, he designed and built an elaborate test rig, which he called an aerodynamometric scale. A 29½-foot-diameter motorized carrousel, it had four crisscross arms upon which Breguet could mount proposed wing sections, rotor blades or fuselage shapes to measure the aerodynamic forces generated by their movement through air. The next year, after much testing of theories and designs, he recruited a small group of investors to fund his research. He also enlisted his brother, Jacques, and Charles Richet, his old mentor, as his main collaborators. And then, late in 1906, he undertook to build his first crude helicopter in a workshop he had rented near the Maison Breguet factory. Powered by a 40-horsepower Antoinette engine, it had a steel tube frame and four rotors (page 28).

Breguet's team of workmen, supervised by an engineer called Volumard, had barely begun their work when Breguet wrote a letter to his brother—who was in Alexandria, Egypt, on company business—that showed he was not ready to concede anything to airplanes. He intended, he said, to outdo the world famous airman Alberto Santos-Dumont, who was then considered the leading contender to collect a 50,000-franc ($10,000) prize offered to the first pilot who could fly his plane around a specified course one kilometer (.62 mile) in length. Named the Deutsch-Archdeacon prize after its two wealthy sponsors, it was the goal of nearly every hopeful aircraft designer.

Breguet's bold ambition did not really seem too farfetched at the time. With the exception of the Wright brothers, who had made flights of more than 38 minutes and 24 miles, no airplane experimenter in the world had yet stayed up for even half a minute or flown even a quarter of the distance required for the coveted prize. The Wrights chose not to compete for the award, and Breguet was confident that he would be able to build an aerial vehicle that would outperform any other aircraft of the day.

Now that his helicopter—which he called a gyroplane—was actually under construction, Breguet's confidence in the project gave him the determination to keep going, even though he could work on it only at night and on weekends. He turned a deaf ear to the rising chorus of pleas from relatives, friends and colleagues to forget about such aeronautical foolishness and content himself with electric motors and his career at Maison Breguet. His superior there, Gaston Sciama—who had been running the company since the death of Louis's father—even told him: "I would rather you become an alcoholic than build aircraft!"

As the machinery took shape and underwent preliminary testing during the spring and summer of 1907, there were some setbacks to contend with. In February, Breguet wrote to his brother: "My 'Gyroplane' advances greatly and I am more and more satisfied." Then he complained that his Antoinette engine, generally regarded as one of the best aircraft engines of his day, was "trash and I have been formidably robbed. I will extricate myself all the same."

In May, two of the craft's rotating wings collided and were heavily damaged, and in June the major fuselage framework collapsed, causing still more costly damage. But to warnings that he risked financial ruin, he replied that to think about "reversing our engines" would be "infantile." Instead, he outlined plans to start a separate company that would begin by turning out 10 gyroplanes a year, selling them at 20,000 francs ($4,000) each.

Finally, on September 29, 1907, the Breguet-Richet Gyroplane No. 1 was wheeled out for a real test in an open field near the factory. As it sat there, its pretensions as a flying machine seemed almost ludicrous. The fragile X-shaped frame stretched out to rest upon support posts at the tips, where four individual 26-foot rotor systems were mounted. Each rotor consisted of four sections of biplane wings, for a total of 32 blades in all. At the center of the frame, alongside the Antoinette engine, sat the slender young engineer Volumard, who had been chosen as pilot—partly because of his loyal work and intimate knowledge of the mechanism, partly because he weighed only 110 pounds and partly because he was brave enough to position himself in the middle of all those flailing blades.

But even with the bantamweight Volumard in the pilot's seat, the craft weighed considerably more than 1,000 pounds, and not even Breguet could entertain any illusions that Gyroplane No. 1 would be able to circle a one-kilometer course. For Breguet had not installed any control system to stabilize it in the air or to make it move horizontally. Instead, four courageous men stood beneath the rotors to help balance the machine by steadying the supports under the tips of the frame.

As Breguet looked on confidently, Volumard revved up the Antoinette and felt the ungainly, quivering machine lift into the air. It was not a true helicopter flight—the pilot could not control his machine—but it was the first time in history that a rotary-winged craft had ever hoisted itself and a human being off the ground. Kept from tipping over by the four men holding the corners, the machine rose to an altitude of about two feet and hovered there for a full minute.

Cheered by this brief confirmation of his rotary system's potential for lift, Breguet went back to his drawing board—and to his aerodynamometric scale—in hopes of building a truly flyable helicopter. Meanwhile, in the Norman town of Lisieux, another French engineer, Paul Cornu, was working just as confidently on his own version of a vertically rising aircraft.

Cornu, too, had been spurred by the prospect of the 50,000-franc prize for a one-kilometer flight. He had built and flown a 28-pound model in 1906. By August of 1907, backed by 125 friends who had risked 100 francs ($20) each, he had a full-scale machine ready for takeoff attempts but prudently tested it first with a 110-pound bag of sand instead of himself.

Cornu's helicopter was far more delicate than Breguet's sprawling rig.

Gyroplane No. 1, designed by Louis Breguet (inset), occupies the yard of his workshop in Douai, France, before its first flight in 1907.

The skeletal frame consisted of a single 20-foot steel tube bent to form a long, wide U. At either end of the arms, fore and aft, was mounted a rotor, which consisted of a wheel with two paddles attached. Just beyond the farthest sweep of each rotor was hung a deflecting panel that could be tilted at different angles in order to use the downward prop wash for stability and horizontal propulsion. The pilot would sit surrounded by working parts—the engine virtually in his lap; the battery under his seat; transmission-pulley wheels, leather drive belts and the whirling tips of the rotors above; and his rudimentary control levers on either side. The whole apparatus, allowing for Cornu, weighed just 573 pounds—less than half as much as Breguet's.

On November 13, 1907, Cornu was set to go. Seating himself in his invention, he ran up the 24-horsepower engine until the rotors were turning at 90 revolutions per minute. Then he found himself hovering about a foot above the ground; for several minutes he hung there, the first human being ever to rise vertically in a powered, heavier-than-air flying machine, completely free of any support from the earth. Later that day, Cornu lifted off again, rising to about five feet. To keep the craft from tipping, Cornu's brother grabbed hold of the frame—and was lifted, too.

Having accomplished the first one-man and two-man ascents in a helicopter, Cornu decided to tether his machine to the ground with safety ropes during future tests. In the next few months he made more than 300 attempts, lifted off about 15 times and managed to move both forward and backward. But his control system was woefully inadequate for purposeful flight—the rotors were simply giant fans and could not be controlled in any effective way—and it was obvious that the craft's delicate design would be no match for the stresses involved in sustained vertical flight.

To the disappointment of both Cornu and Louis Breguet, the Anglo-French aviator Henry Farman circled a one-kilometer course on January 13, 1908, in a spidery fixed-wing biplane and won the tantalizing Deutsch-Archdeacon prize. Even so, Cornu commenced work on a new and different helicopter design. But his funds soon ran out, and he faded from public view.

Undiscouraged by Farman's success, Breguet pressed on with his helicopter research. During 1908, he built two variations of his first machine. These were really hybrids—half-helicopter, half-airplane. Each had a single pair of large, side-by-side rotors tilted toward the front to provide both vertical lift and a forward push. Awkward as these two designs look to a later age, they actually flew, under a degree of control, one going as high as 33 feet.

Then on August 8, 1908—little more than two weeks after Breguet's best flight—Wilbur Wright stunned the French aviation community with a brilliant demonstration of precision flying at a race track near Le Mans. One of those who witnessed the flight was the French aviation pioneer Léon Delagrange. He realized immediately that the Americans were far ahead of their French counterparts in the development of controllable aircraft. "Well, we are beaten!" he said afterward. "We just don't exist." Breguet refused to take so pessimistic a view and maintained a brave front. Two months after the Wright flight at Le Mans, he assured an interviewer: "It will be easy for me to match the records of Wright, Farman and Delagrange." But even the buoyant Breguet now had to face the fact that the airplane had far outpaced the helicopter, and that his work on rotary-winged craft was turning out to be too expensive.

He had been claiming all along that it was "a simple matter" to build fixed-wing airplanes and he soon proved that this boast, at least, was not an idle one. From 1909 onward, Breguet swiftly became one of the world's foremost airplane makers. His obsession with helicopters, if not forgotten, had definitely been put aside. At about the same time that Breguet moved on to airplane manufacturing, however, a young Russian experimenter was diligently pursuing the elusive dream of rotary-winged flight.

In late 1909 and early 1910, residents of the ancient Russian city of Kiev were startled to see a bulky, wedge-shaped object gliding at fearsome speed along the snow-covered streets. In it, grasping a steering wheel,

French mechanic Paul Cornu sits behind the Antoinette engine of his fragile helicopter. The 24-hp unit drove the aircraft's two paddle-shaped rotor blades, which were linked by the belt running over pulleys above Cornu's head.

The skeletal frame of Louis Breguet's Gyroplane No. 2 takes shape in the Breguet workshop. Designed with two 25-foot rotors and biplane wings for good measure, the craft rose to 33 feet on July 22, 1908, but was wrecked in landing.

sat a solemn young man, sometimes accompanied by two or three equally composed companions. Puzzled spectators could see that the thing was clearly a horseless sleigh—driven on its course by a large, engine-powered propeller mounted at the rear.

Igor Ivanovich Sikorsky, the 20-year-old designer and driver of the sleigh, enjoyed his noisy excursions in the incongruous machine, but he regarded his sleighing program as a methodical experiment in aerodynamics; his earthbound forays were designed to expand his knowledge of engines and propellers. His ultimate objective was to ascend into the sky by helicopter.

Sikorsky, the son of one of Russia's foremost medical psychologists, had been studying and dreaming about the challenges of helicopter design for years. Steeped since childhood in the speculations of Jules Verne and Leonardo da Vinci, and more recently inspired by the exploits of Count Ferdinand von Zeppelin and the Wright brothers, he had firmly committed himself to a life of creating flying machines and had chosen the helicopter as the likeliest instrument for his ambition.

When Sikorsky was a child, his gift for creative experiment had occasionally caused minor family problems. The maid refused to clean his room for fear of being poisoned by the chemical compounds that he mixed and cooked up there. And his teen-age sisters were infuriated when their younger brother sneaked into their room and made off with the whalebone stays from their corsets. Strong, slender and springy, the corset stays made ideal bowspring engines for his small helicopter models.

Sikorsky was a talented tinkerer who possessed both mechanical and academic aptitude. He honed his skills during three years in the Russian Naval Academy at St. Petersburg, several months at an engineering school in Paris, and a year and a half at Kiev's Polytechnic Institute. Then, in the summer of 1908, he plunged into full-time aeronautical experimentation.

Early in 1909, financed by an admiring older sister and his father, Sikorsky took the long rail journey back to Paris. There, in a city bubbling with excitement about aviation's bright future, he visited airfields, saw airplanes struggling to fly and ran into the renowned pilot Louis Blériot, who would soon make history by flying 23½ miles across the English Channel in a 540-pound monoplane.

In Paris, Sikorsky also met Captain Ferdinand Ferber, the dean of French fliers, who had been the first Frenchman to grasp the significance of the Wright brothers' achievement. Ferber would become the young Russian's chief aeronautical mentor. Sikorsky recalled that Ferber advised him "again and again, kindly but firmly" not to waste time on helicopters but to stick to the fixed-wing airplane. However, Sikorsky was stubborn, and returning home in the summer of 1909, he built his first helicopter.

Powered by a 25-horsepower motorcycle engine mounted in a boxlike, skeletal wooden frame, the aircraft did not look especially promising. It had two hollow drive shafts (one inside the other), each attached to a pair of horizontal, two-bladed props, one above the other and geared to turn in opposite directions. These were the lifting rotors, and their shafts were guyed in place with a considerable amount of piano wire. Like Louis Breguet's machine that had lifted off in 1907, the Sikorsky craft lacked a control system. If it ascended into the air, the pilot would be unable to stabilize or maneuver it. Sikorsky intended to add controls later; for the present, he was more interested in testing the lifting power of his machine, which he referred to as No. 1.

One July day, with his ungainly craft positioned in the lush green gardens of the family estate, Igor Sikorsky slipped into the pilot's seat and started the engine. The rotors slapped noisily around their shafts. But the drive belt kept slipping, and when Sikorsky adjusted the belt, vibrations shook the machine so alarmingly that he had to cut power. He took the rotors apart, rebalanced them and carefully reinstalled them, but this did not eliminate the problem. Finally, Sikorsky pounded a four-foot length of hardwood into the inner propeller shaft, apparently to stiffen it, and cured the shaking. Sikorsky then tried revving up the engine further.

Sitting soberly behind the wheel of one of his two propeller-driven sleighs, Igor Sikorsky takes a few associates for a ride in 1912. The young engineer had built the sleighs two years earlier in hopes of gaining insight into the problems of aerodynamics.

Encouraged by the clouds of dust and leaves billowed about by the whirling rotors, Sikorsky opened the throttle wide. But instead of rising, the helicopter started to tip over. Sikorsky, sensing disaster, leaped onto the framework and at the same time reduced the power. Under his weight, No. 1 slowly righted itself, but even as it straightened, Sikorsky could feel the lifting force. His helicopter acted as if it wanted to rise.

During the next two months, Sikorsky tinkered and tested from early morning far into the night. The helicopter waltzed and skittered awkwardly across the ground but failed to rise. Sikorsky adjusted the piano wires to alter the pitch of the paddles and reinforced or changed other parts. Eventually, he got his machine to perform more obediently—and at full throttle—for minutes at a time. But at best it was still unstable, and the machine's maximum lifting power was obviously far short of that needed to lift itself, let alone a pilot.

Sikorsky soon gave up hope of ever flying No. 1 and decided to convert it into a stationary test stand. After anchoring the craft to a large weight scale, he was able to measure its precise lifting power— 357 pounds, or approximately 100 pounds less than its own weight without any fuel or a pilot. With the apparatus safely tied down, he ran a series of experiments using various combinations of rotor blades. Finally, in October 1909, he dismantled No. 1; all his thoughts were now focused on No. 2, which he determined to build after several months of careful planning.

On a trip to Paris, Sikorsky purchased two more motorcycle engines, one of 15 horsepower and the other a 25-horsepower model. He tried these on his propeller-driven sleighs. Dividing his time between sleigh test rides, making sketches of aircraft designs and constructing helicopter models, he plotted his strategy until February of 1910. Then he removed the large engine from the wedge-shaped sleigh and began to build his second helicopter. In a few weeks it was ready. Cleaner of line and more graceful than his first machine, No. 2 towered three times as tall as the bearded young inventor. Like its predecessor, it had two contrarotating lifting propellers—but this time, each prop consisted of three delicate strut-and-canvas airfoil blades instead of crude wooden paddles.

Tests soon showed that No. 2 could almost hoist its entire 400-pound bulk, and Sikorsky thought that with further modification the machine might even lift off the ground. But a machine that just barely achieved a tiny hop, like those of Breguet and Cornu more than two years before, would not be a genuine flying craft. Sikorsky now realized that even after spending a considerable amount of his family's money, he still knew too little about helicopters to build and fly a true one. He had nevertheless confronted some of the basic obstacles to rotary-winged flight—inadequate lift, destructive vibra-

Outside his father's house in Kiev in 1910, young Sikorsky stands ready to make adjustments on his second helicopter. Rebuilt from a vibration-plagued 1909 model, the new, lighter craft resembled, in Sikorsky's words, "a huge butterfly." It could lift its weight—400 pounds—but nothing more: no fuel to sustain flight, no pilot.

tions and the need for lighter, more durable materials. The problem of how to control attitude, altitude and motion if the machine even left the ground also eluded him.

Sikorsky's confidence that a practical helicopter would be built someday had not faltered. But he knew that he could not do it in 1910. He tore down No. 2, salvaged the engine and turned to the construction of fixed-wing airplanes. Within months, he took his first flight—as the pilot of an airplane. By 1913 his 9,000-pound *Bolshoi-Baltisky*—the first four-engined plane in the world—was flying before the eyes of his amazed and admiring Czar. But the War was to come, followed by the Russian Revolution. Not for decades would Sikorsky attempt to build another helicopter.

In the years that followed Sikorsky's first efforts, numerous other experimenters in several nations—obsessed with the notion of the helicopter—continued to build powered vehicles designed to lift vertically into the air. In Denmark, Jacob C. H. Ellehammer managed in 1912 to rise briefly from the ground in an odd but graceful little helicopter with stubby rotor blades attached to the edge of two disks spinning in opposite directions, one above the other. Ellehammer's craft had a conventional propeller to provide forward thrust, but it never rose higher than about four feet—not enough to try out the secondary function of the large lower rotor disk, which was covered with cloth in hopes that it could double as a parachute, ballooning if the engine were suddenly to fail.

In the United States, Emile Berliner, a German immigrant and an energetic inventor, produced with his son Henry an awkward machine that managed to get three or four feet off the ground. The Berliners then went on to construct a strange craft that vaguely resembled the German Fokker triplane of military fame. It had two overhead rotors, conventional rudder-and-elevator tail surfaces plus a small vertical rotor on the fuselage to lift the tail, and a winglike control panel between the wheels of the landing gear. This aerial conglomerate flew many times, covering as much as 100 yards at a time and staying aloft one and one half minutes. But like all those craft that preceded it, it was not really controllable.

In the early 1920s, as Emile Berliner futilely attempted to perfect his machine, the United States Army was funding the experiments of George de Bothezat, a refugee from revolution-torn Russia. De Bothezat, a prolific writer and lecturer on the theory of rotary-winged flight, had unbounded faith in his own abilities. "I am," he once said, "the world's greatest scientist and outstanding mathematician." Working at McCook Field in Dayton, Ohio, he put together a maze of pipes and guy wires and gears and 38 rotor blades. The engine and four lifting rotors were mounted on a cross-shaped frame. Called by some the "Flying Octopus," the helicopter had two control wheels as well as a control stick and pedals, which enabled

A crowd gathers under the huge wings of George Clout's helicopter, patterned after a model the inventor saw in a toyshop.

Before the experiments of such men as Louis Breguet and Paul Cornu convincingly demonstrated the value of proceeding according to sound aerodynamic principles, various amateur inventors and even some respected scientists labored for years to construct vertical-flight machines whose fanciful designs defied all known physical laws. A few of these odd birds may have hopped, skipped or jumped a bit, but not one of them ever truly ascended into the sky. Several of the strangest specimens are shown on these pages.

The machine above, devised by English inventor George Clout in 1903, had 30-foot wings that were supposed to revolve around a circular rail above the engine. It resembled nothing so much as an enormous mechanical butterfly. After failing to win military support for his idea, Clout was unable to go on and abandoned the project in 1904.

Other enthusiasts followed with even more bizarre contraptions. In 1910, the local blacksmith of Jetmore, Kansas, one A. E. Hunt, constructed a spectacular whirligig with two cylindrical disks to serve as rotors. It raised a few eyebrows, but that was about all. Meanwhile, in Chicago, James F. Scott, a builder of theatrical scenery by profession, took up constructing aeronautical devices as a hobby. His brain child had no fewer than 16 disks, which, when moved up and down by a lightweight engine, were supposed to hoist the craft aloft.

Perhaps the best-known of the early experimenters was Wilbur R. Kimball, who, by the time he unveiled his first flying machine in 1908, was already an established electrical engineer and a founding member of the American Aero Club. His ambitious helicopter, with its 20 short, three-bladed rotors mounted on a skeletal frame, looked for all the world like an oversized cake mixer—and, alas, flew like one.

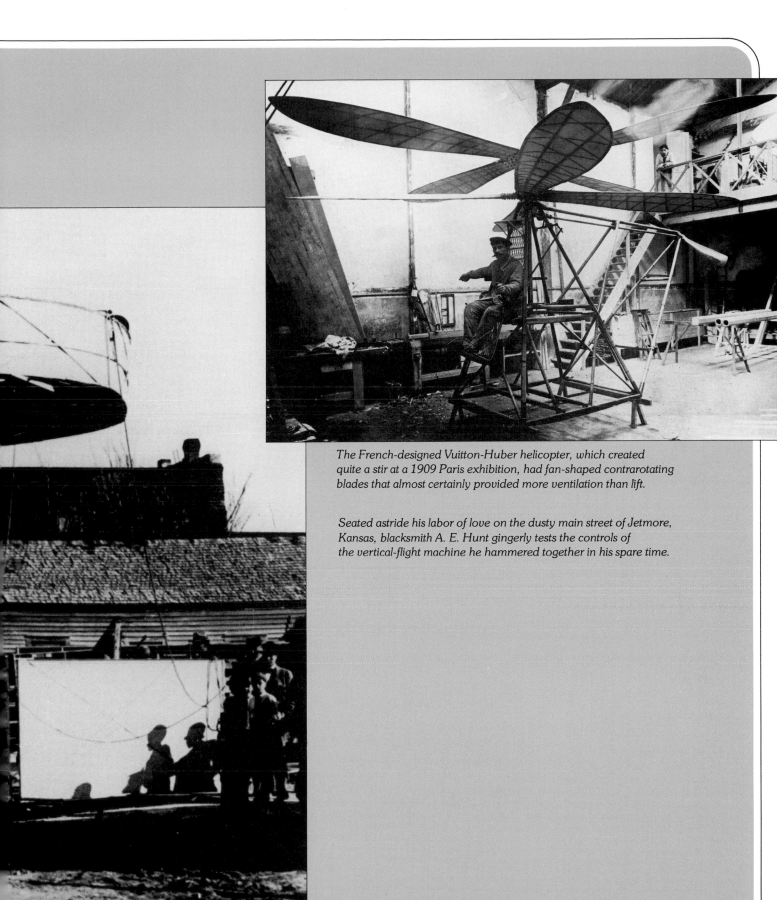

The French-designed Vuitton-Huber helicopter, which created quite a stir at a 1909 Paris exhibition, had fan-shaped contrarotating blades that almost certainly provided more ventilation than lift.

Seated astride his labor of love on the dusty main street of Jetmore, Kansas, blacksmith A. E. Hunt gingerly tests the controls of the vertical-flight machine he hammered together in his spare time.

James Scott's 1910 helicopter managed to flutter and tremble briefly beneath rotors that were about as sturdy as potato chips.

Wilbur Kimball mounts his craft, which was christened by Anna Held, a well-known actress. It refused to fly, despite her blessings.

the pilot to change the pitch, or the angle, of the craft's four rotors.

Powered by its 220-horsepower engine, de Bothezat's machine lifted its 3,600-pound bulk—along with four men clinging to its maze of pipes—and rose to a maximum altitude of 30 feet. But the Army could see no practical use for such a craft and canceled its contract with de Bothezat after spending some $200,000 on his project.

In France, the Spaniard Raul Pateras Pescara experimented with a helicopter having two biplane rotors that spun in opposite directions on concentric shafts. By 1922, his machine could hover for two and a half minutes at more than three feet off the ground, and in 1924, he set a helicopter speed record by flying at eight miles per hour for almost half a mile. On another occasion, he reached an altitude of nearly 30 feet. Though Pescara's craft was an obvious step forward, it too lacked the controls necessary for sustained flight.

Around the same time, French engineer Etienne Oehmichen designed a helicopter that was one of the most promising of the many models that had been built since Sikorsky abandoned his vertical-flight experiments in 1910. Lifted by six large rotors—and using eight smaller propellers for forward movement—this machine had various mechanisms for regulating direction, pitch and roll. It reportedly flew more than 1,000 times, staying up for as long as 14 minutes, reaching a height of 50 feet and flying slightly more than a mile. In 1924, Oehmichen won a 90,000-franc ($4,700) prize offered by the French Air Ministry for the first helicopter flight over a one-kilometer circuit.

But coming as it did at the very time that United States Army Air Service planes were making the first flight around the entire world, Oehmichen's prizewinning hop seemed to be a paltry accomplishment. Indeed, the helicopter had only fallen further and further behind the airplane since the days when men like Sikorsky and Louis Breguet could dream that rotor-powered vehicles might overtake and even supplant fixed-wing aircraft. So formidable were the technical obstacles, in fact, that vertical flight seemed almost to be an idea whose time could never really come. ∿

A strange bird of many wings

Of all the early attempts at controlled rotary-winged flight, the most ambitious by far was that of George de Bothezat, the Russian émigré who built a helicopter for the U.S. Army Air Service. The project got under way in the summer of 1921 at McCook (later Wright) Field in Dayton, Ohio. Working directly from his own theoretical formulations and for the most part disdaining models, wind tunnels and other standard preliminaries, de Bothezat and his crew finished their helicopter in December 1922. The enormous craft that emerged from their zealously patrolled top-secret enclosure resembled a pair of crossed

A dour-looking George de Bothezat sits in a web of struts and cables at the controls of his helicopter. His hand is on the stick that governs the pitch, or angle, of the blades of the four main lifting rotors.

Four 26-foot rotors dominate de Bothezat's blueprint of his helicopter. Each blade was a fabric-covered airfoil. The engine that drove them was anchored at the intersection of the two support beams. The pilot sat facing the engine, in front of the narrow pair of wheels. Two small three-bladed airscrews in the middle helped to cool the engine.

bridge spans with huge ceiling fans at their ends (right). It weighed 3,600 pounds and was powered by a single 180-hp Le Rhône engine.

De Bothezat's creation made more than 100 test flights, once setting a duration record of 2 minutes 45 seconds, and another time reaching an altitude of 30 feet. The proud inventor sent Thomas Edison pictures of the tests, some of which are reproduced in this essay. Edison—who had himself conducted vertical-flight experiments—congratulated the Russian on having produced "the first successful helicopter." But Edison's encomium was premature. De Bothezat's machine could not be fully controlled in flight, and it failed to meet many of the Army's performance specifications. In 1924, having invested $200,000 in the project, the Air Service ordered the effort abandoned and the helicopter dismantled and scrapped.

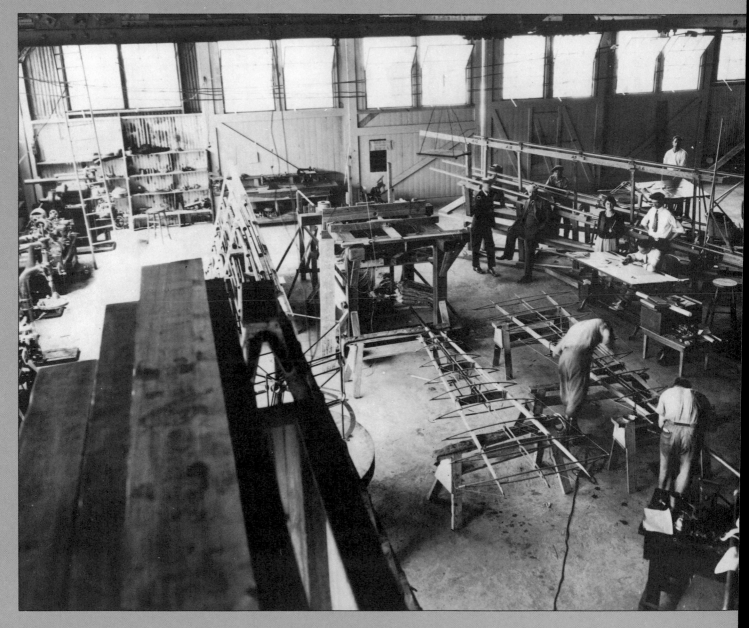

De Bothezat hoists the 25-pound wood-and-steel frame of one of the rotor blades. He claimed that each blade would be able to generate 250 pounds of lift.

Under the watchful eye of de Bothezat (seated at rear with cap), workmen at McCook Field put the finishing touches on a pair of rotor-blade frames.

Hanging from bars that form the central shafts of the rotors, workmen demonstrate the strength of one of the rotor hubs.

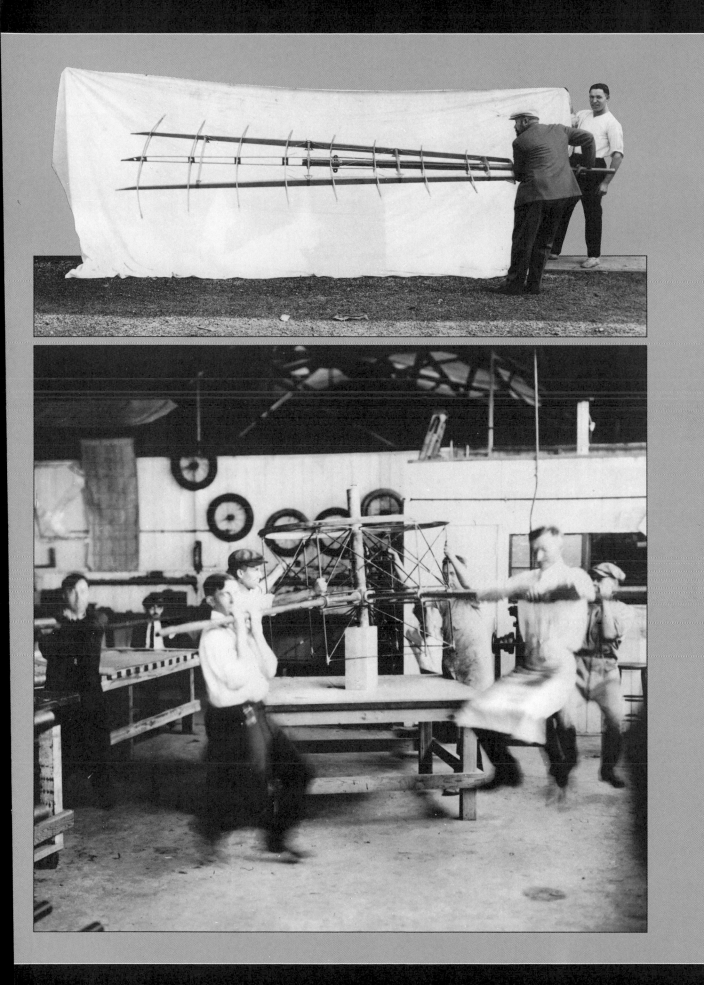

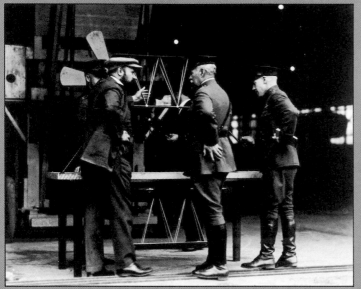

De Bothezat conducts General Billy Mitchell (right) and another officer on a tour of his project headquarters at McCook Field.

As the helicopter's engine is revved up in an early test, workers at McCook Field gather for a look at the ultrasecret craft. The two vertical propellers spinning at the ends of the lateral support beam are for horizontal control; they were later found to be useless and were removed.

Workers stabilize the helicopter as it hovers just above the ground in an early test. Months later the craft made a brief flight with four "passengers" holding on to its struts and supports.

The de Bothezat helicopter dangles a rope used to gauge the craft's altitude— the knots are 10 feet apart. Even at maximum engine speed, the massive lifting rotors turned at just 90 rpm, about half the rate of modern helicopter rotors.

2

The amazing autogiro

he dream of vertical flight might have faded entirely had it not been for a visionary young Spanish aristocrat named Juan de la Cierva who made a breakthrough that brought the elusive helicopter to the threshold of reality. Like other aeronautical enthusiasts of his day, he had become obsessed with flight as a boy. The first airplanes in Spanish skies had arrived from France in 1910, fueling the passion for aviation that was already burning in the 14-year-old la Cierva, son of a former cabinet minister. La Cierva and his teen-age friends had been studiously following the exploits of aviation pioneers and had flown countless model planes and helicopter toys. In 1910 they decided to build a glider big enough to ride.

When launched from a hill by a gang of boys pulling its towrope, the glider and passenger would rise several feet off the ground and come to rest a few yards downhill. One day they decided to reward la Cierva's younger brother for his rope pulling by giving him a ride. He was inexperienced and lighter than the other boys, and his weight, la Cierva later wrote, "upset all my aerodynamic calculations" as the glider shot 50 feet into the air. The boys holding the rope were so startled by the craft's rapid ascent that they neglected to pull on the rope—with the result that the glider "came down in a spin as suddenly as it had gone up." La Cierva thought at first that his little brother was dead, and was greatly relieved to find that he had only been knocked senseless.

But this incident did not deter la Cierva. He analyzed what had happened and came up with a revised set of performance characteristics for the glider. As his knowledge of aerodynamics grew, he turned to ever more ambitious projects. In late 1911, he and two friends began work on a full-sized, engine-driven biplane. To power it, the youngsters had negotiated a deal with Jean Mauvais, a French pilot living in Madrid whose own Sommer biplane lay in a heap, reduced to ruin by a crash. Mauvais had agreed to give the boys his engine and what little else of the wreckage could be salvaged; he also promised that when they finished their plane, he would test-fly it and then give them all flight lessons.

With their power plant assured, la Cierva and his companions forged rapidly ahead. They pieced together a framework for the fuselage and wings. Needing seasoned wood for a new propeller, they found a well-pickled barroom tabletop and carved out an airscrew. They then covered their framework with cheap canvas, doped it with glue to make it airtight, painted it scarlet and christened their handiwork the *Red Crab*.

"The wings of tomorrow" is how Spanish inventor Juan de la Cierva referred to his autogiro, seen here in a 1928 British illustration. La Cierva prophesied that the craft would "deliver far places from loneliness, and make near neighbors of the communities of a continent."

Amazingly, the contraption flew, and flew well. During the next year or so Mauvais made many flights with a passenger squeezed in behind him. He frequently took la Cierva up for a spin and let him reach around to hold the wheel. But to the boys' grave disappointment, the Frenchman never came through on his promise to make them pilots.

Even so, they had much to be proud of. The *Red Crab* was remarkable enough for having been patched together by a trio of teenagers. More astonishing, it was almost surely the first Spanish-built plane to fly successfully. Its demise was as special as its beginning. Every time it rained the *Red Crab* grew sticky all over—the glue was rinsing out. Finally the scarlet-oozing craft just disintegrated into a pile of wreckage. The trio next built a monoplane, which flew with middling success. But a series of accidents involving costly repairs paid for by the parents led eventually to the abandonment of the plane and the breakup of the trio.

La Cierva did not lose his youthful enthusiasm for aviation. In 1919, after finishing a six-year civil engineering course, he and some backers—who sank 150,000 pesetas ($30,000) into the project—built a large trimotor bomber, aiming at a 30,000-peseta ($6,000) prize from the Army and possible future contracts. The plane flew well once. But then, during a second flight, an Army pilot unfamiliar with such large craft crashed after a low-altitude stall. He was only bruised, but the bomber was ruined—along with all hopes of winning the competition.

La Cierva blamed pilot error alone for the mishap and would not concede any flaws in his design. However, the bomber was the last ordinary aircraft he would ever design or build. His life soon entered a new phase, during which he abandoned for a brief period any direct involvement in aeronautics. Marrying in 1919 and taking up a career similar to his father's, la Cierva became a deputy in the national parliament. But his mind, trained for engineering problems and mathematical analysis, remained occupied with aviation, and with what he now saw as a crucial flaw in all airplanes: A fixed-wing craft, he reasoned, could achieve safety only with speed, since the movement of its wings through the air provided its sole support. Perhaps the helicopter offered the solution to the problem of achieving safe, sustained flight at any speed.

But the continuing failures of helicopter experimenters soon convinced la Cierva that the helicopter concept had too many inherent mechanical complexities to be the answer. For example, a helicopter design that started out simply, with an engine turning a rotor, immediately had to be made more complicated to deal with the problem of torque, which would whirl the rotor in one direction while spinning the fuselage in the other. Unlike other experimenters, however, la Cierva did not believe that sheer mechanical ingenuity would lead directly to a practical helicopter. Instead, he racked his brain until he came up with the essential halfway step, an airplane with whirling overhead wings.

La Cierva found the basic clue to his new concept by contemplating the behavior of simple helicopter toys, primarily as they floated lazily down from their zenith, their rotors having reversed direction as they

The dynamics of rotary-winged flight

What makes a vertical flying machine rise into the air? The rotor blades of an autogiro or a helicopter are airfoils much like the fixed wings of an airplane, and they function in much the same way. All three types of aircraft are kept aloft by lift created when their airfoils pass rapidly through the air. The shape and tilt of the airfoils cause air streaming over the top of them to travel farther and faster than the air flowing beneath them *(right)*. The speed of the air over the top reduces air pressure on the upper surface, while the air striking the bottom surface increases pressure there. This difference in pressure creates lift; if the force of the lift is greater than the weight of the airfoils and the fuselage to which they are attached, the craft will rise.

The faster an airfoil moves through the air, the more lift it creates. The autogiro's rotor blades offer an advantage over the fixed wing of an airplane in that the rotor blades move rapidly through the air, even while the craft itself is moving slowly. An early autogiro like the one shown at bottom right could thus take off and stay aloft at forward speeds as low as 20 mph, about a third of the forward speed needed by an airplane of approximately the same size.

Even an autogiro, however, requires some forward speed—provided by its engine and propeller—to keep its rotor revolving by autorotation *(right)*. If the engine stops, the autogiro will begin to descend, but air passing upward around the blades keeps the rotor turning slowly, ensuring a gentle downward drift.

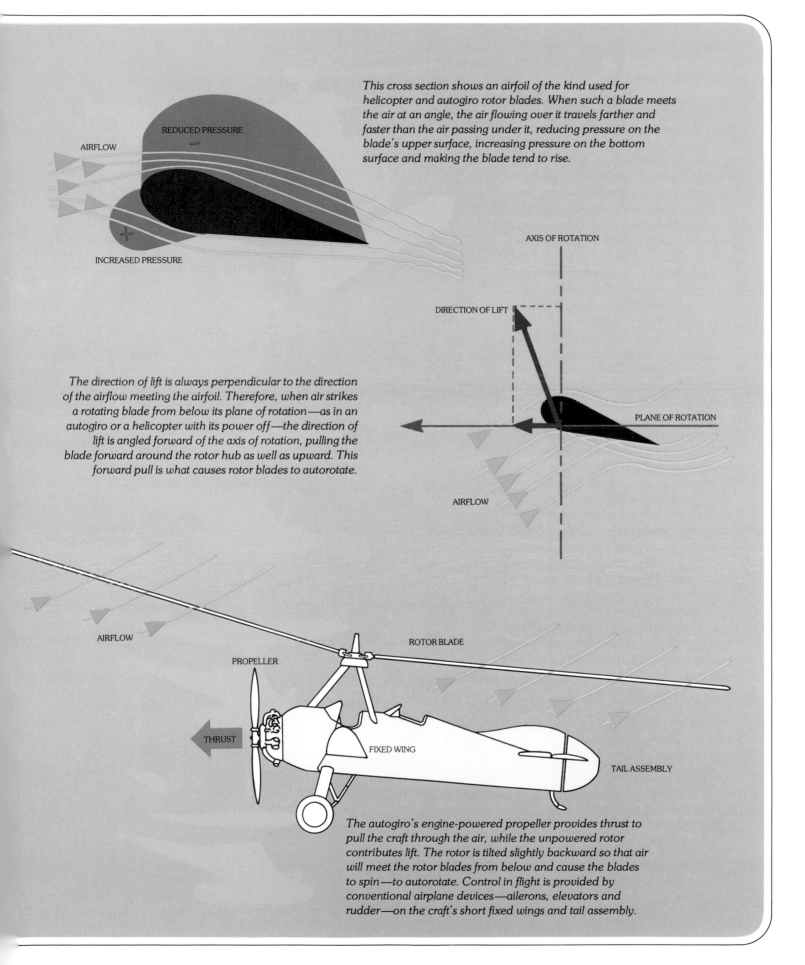

This cross section shows an airfoil of the kind used for helicopter and autogiro rotor blades. When such a blade meets the air at an angle, the air flowing over it travels farther and faster than the air passing under it, reducing pressure on the blade's upper surface, increasing pressure on the bottom surface and making the blade tend to rise.

REDUCED PRESSURE

AIRFLOW

INCREASED PRESSURE

AXIS OF ROTATION

DIRECTION OF LIFT

PLANE OF ROTATION

AIRFLOW

The direction of lift is always perpendicular to the direction of the airflow meeting the airfoil. Therefore, when air strikes a rotating blade from below its plane of rotation—as in an autogiro or a helicopter with its power off—the direction of lift is angled forward of the axis of rotation, pulling the blade forward around the rotor hub as well as upward. This forward pull is what causes rotor blades to autorotate.

AIRFLOW

ROTOR BLADE

PROPELLER

THRUST

FIXED WING

TAIL ASSEMBLY

The autogiro's engine-powered propeller provides thrust to pull the craft through the air, while the unpowered rotor contributes lift. The rotor is tilted slightly backward so that air will meet the rotor blades from below and cause the blades to spin—to autorotate. Control in flight is provided by conventional airplane devices—ailerons, elevators and rudder—on the craft's short fixed wings and tail assembly.

Controlling a helicopter in flight

Flying a helicopter is far more difficult than flying a plane, since it involves constant use of both hands and both feet.

Using his left hand, the pilot adjusts the overall lifting power of the rotor with the collective pitch lever *(right)*. Pitch is the angle at which a blade is set to meet the air. In general, the higher the pitch, the greater the lift. The pilot raises or lowers the lever to increase or reduce simultaneously the pitch of all the blades.

The handle of the collective lever is the throttle; it turns like a motorcycle's throttle. The pilot uses it to feed more fuel when increasing pitch in order to climb, less when hovering or descending. His aim is to maintain constant rotor rpm regardless of pitch, since rotors and engines operate most efficiently at a fixed rate of speed. (Most modern helicopters can adjust fuel supply automatically.)

With his right hand, the pilot manipulates the cyclic pitch control stick governing the helicopter's horizontal movements. Moving the stick from its neutral position changes the pitch of each rotor blade cyclically as it rotates, increasing pitch to a maximum value at one point in the rotation and smoothly reducing it to a minimum at the opposite side of the circle. The pitch adjustments make the blades rise and fall as they rotate; the effect is to tilt the rotor's plane of rotation, or disk, so that some of the rotor's lift operates in a horizontal rather than a vertical direction—that is, some of the lift becomes thrust. Moving the cyclic stick to the right, for example, alters pitch so that the whole rotor disk tilts right and produces thrust in that direction.

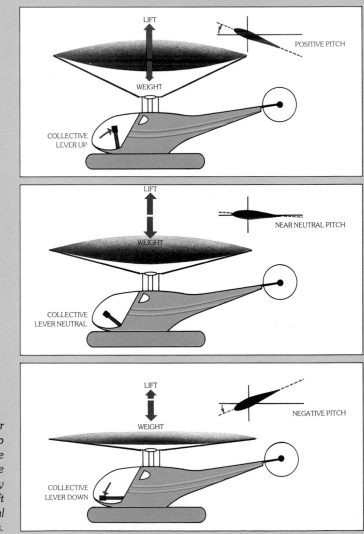

The helicopter's collective lever and cyclic stick control the pitch of the blades of its main rotor; its two pedals control the tail rotor's pitch. These pitch controls and the throttle, the handle of the collective lever, govern all the craft's movements.

MAIN ROTOR

CYCLIC STICK

THROTTLE

COLLECTIVE LEVER

TAIL-ROTOR PEDALS

FUSELAGE

TAIL ROTOR

LIFT

POSITIVE PITCH

WEIGHT

COLLECTIVE LEVER UP

LIFT

NEAR NEUTRAL PITCH

WEIGHT

COLLECTIVE LEVER NEUTRAL

LIFT

NEGATIVE PITCH

WEIGHT

COLLECTIVE LEVER DOWN

The three drawings at right show how the collective pitch lever controls the lifting force of the main rotor. When the lever is up (top), positive rotor pitch creates enough lift to overcome the aircraft's weight, and if the engine can maintain rotor rpm, the helicopter rises. With the lever in neutral (center), the slightly positive pitch is just enough to balance the weight, and the craft hovers. With the lever down (bottom) and the blade pitch neutral or negative, weight exceeds lift and the helicopter descends.

The cyclic pitch stick alters the pitch of each rotor blade individually as it goes through its cycle of rotation. The effect is to tilt the rotor disk in the direction in which the stick is moved, creating horizontal thrust and causing the helicopter to move in that direction. When the rotor disk is tilted sharply during acceleration, the fuselage tilts the same way because the helicopter's center of gravity tends to align itself with the rotor's line of lift.

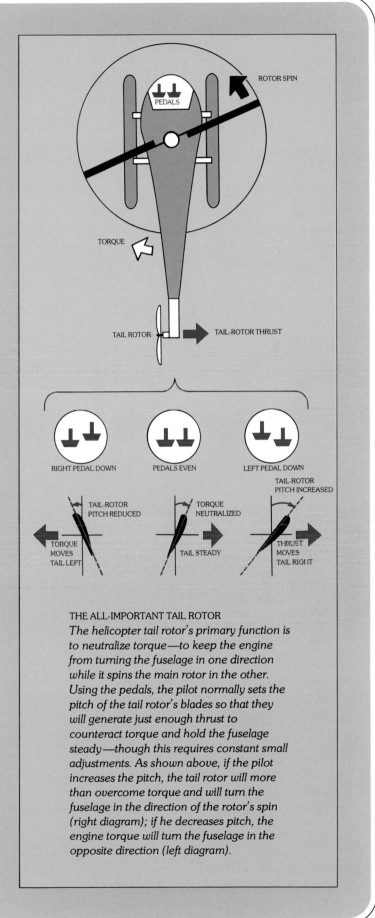

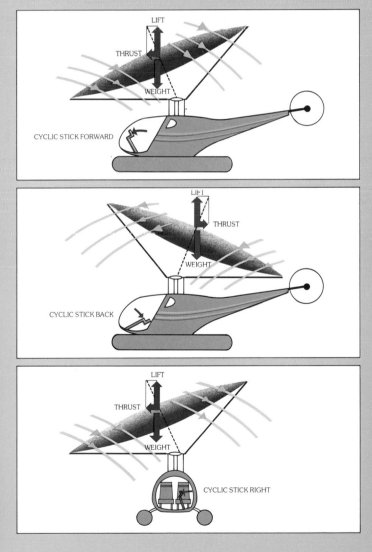

THE ALL-IMPORTANT TAIL ROTOR

The helicopter tail rotor's primary function is to neutralize torque—to keep the engine from turning the fuselage in one direction while it spins the main rotor in the other. Using the pedals, the pilot normally sets the pitch of the tail rotor's blades so that they will generate just enough thrust to counteract torque and hold the fuselage steady—though this requires constant small adjustments. As shown above, if the pilot increases the pitch, the tail rotor will more than overcome torque and will turn the fuselage in the direction of the rotor's spin (right diagram); if he decreases pitch, the engine torque will turn the fuselage in the opposite direction (left diagram).

reached the top of their flight. Partly through his technical knowledge and partly by inspiration, he came to realize that a properly designed rotary wing, if set to spinning in a forward direction, could be made to fly into the wind and provide lift much like an ordinary airplane wing. And as long as the wing was moving through the air—whether sinking through the sky or being pulled forward by an ordinary engine-powered propeller—its turning and lifting would continue.

The principle behind the phenomenon that la Cierva hoped to exploit came to be known as autorotation. Like many other key discoveries, it was basically an ancient idea, but its aeronautical implications had not been fully appreciated. Sailors had long known how to tack into the wind; and windmill builders had found that they could play off the lift produced by a rotating blade against its air resistance to provide rotation in the direction needed. Gliders and planes with their engines off utilized the same phenomenon; while their forward speed maintained lift, their weight offset drag. La Cierva's genius lay in his ability to understand that the same forces that acted on a fixed wing would also act on rotating wings. And although these forces were well known—lift, drag, thrust and weight—it was his application of them that would be so novel.

La Cierva took out a patent on his rotating wings about a year after his trimotor bomber crashed, and coined a name for the new kind of craft he visualized: autogiro, or self-rotator. He began almost at once to build a full-sized model, confident that what looked so good on paper would actually fly. To a conventional, though wingless, airplane fuselage, he added a rotor, an engine and a propeller. While the engine would power the craft, it would not drive the rotor, which would spin of its own accord and provide lift as the autogiro flew through the air.

As an engineer, la Cierva knew that the freewheeling, unpowered rotor would automatically eliminate torque, which, of course, was one of the most vexing problems of helicopter design. And since there was no torque, the fuselage would not rotate in a direction opposite to that of the rotor. But he also knew that two major problems would remain. The first was gyroscopic resistance of the spinning rotor to being tilted in any direction out of the plane of its rotation. The second was the inequality of lift between the rotor blades as they advanced into the airstream on one side of the craft and then retreated on the other side. Since lift varies as a function of speed, the faster-moving blades on the advancing side of the rotor would create more lift, causing the craft to tilt.

La Cierva's first solution was dazzlingly simple. Instead of using a single four-bladed rotor, as originally envisioned, he installed two rotors, one above the other. With their blades angled to turn in opposite directions, the twin rotors promised to compensate for each other and cancel out the dual problems of gyroscopic resistance and unequal lift.

By October 1920, la Cierva had his creation—which he proudly labeled the C.1—ready for a trial at an airfield near Madrid. His brother-in-law, an artillery captain, had agreed to serve as test pilot. But a brisk taxiing run around the field was enough to show that something was wrong. The rotors whirled as they should, but only one side of the craft's landing gear would leave the ground. If more lift were attained, the autogiro would obviously tip over before it could get aloft. La Cierva quickly realized that the bottom rotor's turning speed—and therefore its lifting power—was cut to about half by the upper rotor's downwash, causing the machine to tilt. He also realized that, in seeking to solve a problem, he had been caught up in the same chain of multiplied complexities that had made him reject the pure helicopter approach.

Learning from his experience, la Cierva started over, using a different fuselage, a more powerful engine and a single rotor. To combat the problem of unequal lift, he used a cam arrangement to change the blades' angle of attack as they advanced and retreated around their hub. But this proved ineffective; like C.1, the second autogiro lifted only one wheel and threatened to topple over. Determined to overcome this problem, la Cierva tried yet again, seeking to counter the unbalanced lift with large ailerons on the fuselage and a single main rotor with five blades braced with high-tensile steel wire. This third machine actually hopped off the runway but had to be set right back down—it was clearly fated to succumb to the capsizing forces that had dogged its predecessors. In another trial, it tipped far enough to crumple its blades.

While testing his first autogiros, la Cierva also experimented with scale models powered by rubber bands. One model, its rotor blades made of rattan, performed beautifully. To la Cierva, this was a baffling contradiction—his autogiro concept worked in miniature but in full-sized machines promised only disaster. Then, while attending a performance of the opera *Aïda,* he had a flash of insight. It dawned on him that the model autogiro's rattan rotor blades were flexible. This let each advancing blade, as it acquired excess lift from its increased speed, ride higher until it flattened out relative to the onrushing wind, presenting a less efficient angle of attack and automatically reducing lift. At the same time, the retreating blade dipped, increasing lift. But rattan was unsuitable for a full-sized rotor; la Cierva would need a substitute for its natural flexibility. His solution: On his next full-sized autogiro, he attached each rotor blade to the rotor hub with an angled hinge that let the blade flap freely up or down, tilting to allow the blade to find its own best angle. The centrifugal force of rotation flattened the blades and balanced out the lift. The result: a beautifully simple, self-compensating mechanism.

By January 9, 1923, la Cierva's fourth autogiro had passed its taxi trials and was ready for a test flight. An Army flier, Lieutenant Alejandro Gomez Spencer, was in the cockpit of C.4 as the little craft took off and flew smoothly across the airfield with its hinged blades automatically adjusting their angles and balancing the lift as they turned. He brought the craft down for a smooth landing. Within a few weeks Spencer flew the same C.4 around a circuit for four minutes.

La Cierva continued to tinker with his design. And then, on December 12, 1924, another Army pilot flew the improved model from Cuatro Vientos Airdrome, near Madrid, to a landing field in the town of Getafe.

Juan de la Cierva holds one of the flying models he used to study the aerodynamics of autogiro flight. Built with rotors of lightweight rattan, the model gave him the solution to the autogiro puzzle: The flexible rotors adjusted to changing airflow, making stable, level flight possible.

The distance was only seven miles, and the feat posed no threat to the long-distance flight records of the day. Even so, it was an epochal event, for it marked the first cross-country flight by a craft with whirling wings.

By the summer of 1925, la Cierva had lined up the first customer for his machine: The British Air Ministry was interested in buying two autogiros, but only if la Cierva could demonstrate that they were more versatile than conventional fixed-wing airplanes. Unfortunately, his Spanish test pilots had not progressed much beyond conservative low-level flights, and the autogiro had yet to prove its full capabilities. La Cierva would need a highly skilled and venturesome pilot to put the craft through its paces and show its advantages to potential purchasers.

He found such a flier in Frank Courtney, a test pilot for the British de Havilland Aircraft Company. Gawky and bespectacled, Courtney was so adept at handling experimental aircraft that he was known as the "Man with the Magic Hands." But when he met la Cierva, he was dubious about the bizarre craft with overhead blades instead of wings.

Courtney had already seen an autogiro, but not in flight. A few weeks before, when he was delivering a plane to Spanish officials at Cuatro Vientos, some Army aviators had taken him to a hangar where one of la Cierva's creations was housed. Despite all assurances, Courtney had

Test pilot Frank Courtney, at right, wearing goggles and flight cap, talks with newsmen and officials at Farnborough, England, before taking Juan de la Cierva's sixth autogiro on a demonstration flight. The men on the left had to haul on the cable attached to the rotor to start the blades whirling.

The crowd at Farnborough watches as la Cierva's odd bird rises into the sky. Amazed by its ascent, one of the world's foremost aerodynamicists later commented to test pilot Courtney, "I told you, Frank, that the thing couldn't fly. I still don't believe it. What have you got up your sleeve?"

failed to see how the wingless oddity could get aloft by means of the four rotor blades that drooped above its fuselage. But now, as la Cierva explained how his autogiro worked, the test pilot became convinced that the earnest young Spaniard had made the most important aeronautical breakthrough since the Wright brothers' first flight. Courtney eagerly agreed to try his magic hands at the controls of the novel craft.

The first peculiarity that Courtney had to face was la Cierva's method of getting the rotor to turn rapidly enough to keep going by autorotation. A crew of men would pull on a rope wrapped around knobs on the four rotor blades, after which Courtney would rev up the engine-driven nose prop and careen down the runway until the rotor developed enough lift for takeoff. Once up, however, the machine was in its element, and Courtney soon got used to the unusual feeling of flying wingless, held in the sky only by what he called "the foggy disk of the blades rotating over my head." Before the first day was over, he found that he could land on a preselected spot with almost no roll forward.

By October, Courtney was ready to perform for the British officials, who had specified an exacting series of tests. Courtney flew through most of the prescribed maneuvers without difficulty. But he still had to try the most demanding test, a nearly vertical descent from about 1,500 feet, with power to the nose prop shut down. Partly for fear of damaging the craft before the official demonstration, he had not attempted this difficult stunt during his practice runs.

As la Cierva and the British observers watched, Courtney reached his altitude and shut off the engine. For more than 1,000 feet he sank through the air, slowed by his windmilling rotor blades. Then he realized that he was going down much too fast to make a safe landing. He had been in airplane crashes before, and now he braced himself for one more. The craft hit the ground on its landing gear, which crumpled. Courtney's seat gave way, and he recalled later that he was "jarred as though the world's biggest elephant had given me a swift kick in the behind." But much of the shock had been absorbed by the crumpling landing gear, and the fuselage remained upright while the rotor continued to revolve above the shaken pilot's head. As Courtney stepped stiffly from the cockpit, a crowd of onlookers rushed to greet him.

Despite this heavy landing, the Air Ministry officials deemed the autogiro to have passed all tests. La Cierva got his first contract and made England the base for his future work. Public acclaim and scientific awards poured in. With Courtney in the cockpit la Cierva showed off his invention to the King and Queen and, taking it to the Continent, to officials in France, Belgium and Italy. And then, at Berlin's Tempelhof Airdrome in September 1926, the first hint of real trouble appeared.

The autogiro had been uncrated and assembled, and Courtney took it up for a check flight before his demonstration. Back on the ground, he noticed that every blade was bent slightly out of line at the root. Courtney had proposed earlier that the blades be given a second set of hinges to allow them horizontal as well as vertical play; the movement of the blades back and forth in a horizontal plane would balance the drag forces. La Cierva rejected the idea. When he was shown the deformed blade roots, he insisted that they had been damaged in shipping. The rotors were quickly changed, and the demonstration went on. Courtney, whose perception was based on his pilot's intuition, rather than a knowledge of engineering, deferred to his employer's opinion.

The deformation of the blades had no immediate effect on the craft's performance, but it eventually brought disaster—and proved that a wise designer listens to his test pilots. While cruising at about 1,000 feet over Hamble, England, in February 1927, Courtney noticed an odd groaning sound coming from the rotor. When he cut the engine for a normal autorotational descent, the sound increased and the autogiro began to shake. Courtney eased the nose down to reduce the angle at which the blades met the air. The craft seemed to fly better for a while. But at 200 feet, one blade broke completely off; the vibration increased alarmingly and the three-bladed cripple plummeted down. Just before impact, a second blade snapped off and the autogiro smashed heavily into the ground. Courtney escaped with some broken ribs, a concussion and bruises. Visiting his test pilot in the hospital, la Cierva assured him the extra hinges would be added to the blades. But Courtney had had enough; he quit his job with la Cierva and returned to airplanes.

Once the blades were permitted to flap freely in all directions, the autogiro passed beyond the experimental stage and became a practical flying machine, paving the way for successful helicopters to come. La Cierva's own manufacturing company in England—which would build more than 90 of the craft—could not keep pace with world demand, and in the late 1920s the inventor began to grant production licenses to foreign manufacturers. In Japan, 240 autogiros would eventually be produced, more than in any other country. German, Russian and French companies bought rights to the craft; airplane builder Harold Pitcairn purchased the United States franchise and turned out 58 autogiros before sublicensing the brothers Roderick G. and W. Wallace Kellett—who turned out another 22 of the machines.

The odd craft, often called a "flying windmill," caused a sensation wherever it appeared. La Cierva himself finally took flight lessons and emerged as a star pilot of his own creation. On September 18, 1928, he became the first pilot to cross the English Channel by autogiro, and before long completed a 3,000-mile demonstration trip all over Europe. He had to make many emergency landings but was able to set down so gently that the mishaps only reinforced his claims of autogiro safety.

The craft was put to many practical applications. In the United States, the New Jersey State Forest Service used an autogiro to fight fires in the

Drawing a crowd of curious bystanders, Juan de la Cierva's battered autogiro rests on its side at Paris' Le Bourget field after landing with a damaged wheel. La Cierva and his good-humored passenger, New York journalist Leland Stowe, who inscribed the picture, climbed from the wreckage without a scratch. Had la Cierva crashed in a regular airplane with a higher landing speed, he noted proudly later, he would not have been able to walk away from the accident quite so easily.

Selling America on the Model T of the air

"This year own and enjoy a Pitcairn Autogiro," urged the copy accompanying these advertisements promoting the epitome of high life. Even though the year was 1932 and American purchasing power had been drastically curtailed by the Great Depression, Harold Pitcairn, whose aircraft company held the U.S. rights to the Cierva autogiro, was convinced that the public's enthusiasm for the autogiro could be converted into sales. It was his fond belief that in the PA-18 Tandem sports model, starting at $5,000, he had the Model T of the air.

Pitcairn launched a major campaign to lure well-heeled customers seeking a safe, convenient way to get around— and to get away from it all. Careful to avoid any wild claims, he stressed safety and reliability as the 1,310-pound craft's key features. Although nearly every ad and brochure noted that the Tandem, with its 160-hp engine, could fly through the air at 100 mph, the copy also emphasized the pilot's "ability to descend slower than a man in a parachute, and to come down nearly straight or to glide forward, even in the case of engine failure."

Pitcairn's claims notwithstanding, the autogiro was not as safe as touted. Even experienced hands had trouble flying it; no less a pilot than Amelia Earhart crashed twice. Cracked undercarriages, crumpled wings and broken rotor blades made for costly repairs—new blades could come to $1,000. The bad name the autogiro was getting, coupled with the effects of the advancing Depression, led Pitcairn to withdraw it from the market in 1933, but not without promising to iron out the kinks and return with an improved model. He was as good as his word, but the new craft was never a commercial success.

"Perhaps the courtyard here may permit the Pitcairn Autogiro to taxi closer to the door than on most estates," said this 1932 ad, "yet many country estates have ample room upon the lawn."

"The very isolation of the hunting or fishing camp makes it hard to reach and infrequently enjoyed." But with an autogiro, "starting point and destination are nearer than by any other means."

"The open areas surrounding almost any country club," noted the caption for this illustration, "offer room for the owner of the Pitcairn Autogiro to fly direct to his golf game."

Pine Barrens. Business corporations flew them to promote chewing gum, spark plugs, coal and anything else they had to sell. The *Detroit News* and the *Des Moines Register & Tribune* each had one to cover special stories; the craft were also used for archeological surveys, crop-dusting and just for fun. The 83-year-old Thomas Edison, whose helicopter experiments of half a century before had come to nothing, was treated to a special autogiro demonstration at the Newark, New Jersey, airport. After watching the machine fly as slow as 20 miles per hour and as fast as 115 miles per hour and then alight vertically without rolling a foot, the inventor patted the craft's flexible rotor and exclaimed: "That's the answer! That's the answer!"

The autogiro seemed endlessly adaptable. Once, when Pitcairn's test pilot, James G. Ray, was caught by a dangerous storm, he set down and motored along a highway until the storm passed and it was safe to take off again. If ever proof was needed of the craft's utility, this was it—and the public took note. The craft also won official recognition, and in April 1931, a distinguished group that included Orville Wright gathered on the South Lawn of the White House to watch President Herbert C. Hoover present the Collier Trophy to Harold Pitcairn for "the greatest achievement in aviation"—bringing la Cierva's flying windmill to the United States. As the guests looked into the sky, an autogiro piloted by Ray fluttered out of the blue and came to a gentle landing beside them.

Swift and nimble, the autogiro was one of the few bright spots in the gray times of the Great Depression. Its unique feats amazed people, and the still-unperfected helicopter was all but forgotten. Meanwhile, la Cierva and some of the other builders, particularly Pitcairn, kept tinkering with the autogiro. The clumsy rope-pull start-up of the rotor, for example, clearly had to go.

The first improvement was to provide tail flaps that could deflect the nose prop's upward backwash to get the rotor going. Better still was a simple gear and clutch that connected the engine to the rotor to rev it up for takeoff; the mechanism would then be disconnected. A far more significant advance was la Cierva's development of a system that enabled the pilot to control the pitch of the blades collectively, or all at once. This led, in 1933, to direct-start gearing and pitch control, which were combined in a "jump-start" autogiro that made previous models obsolete. The rotor could now be turned up by engine power to a high rate, but with the blades too flat to lift; when declutched, the blades bit suddenly into the air and the autogiro would jump almost vertically into the air, rising high enough for the prop to pull it forward into regular flight before it sank back down. The blades were then returned to their original pitch and the autogiro flew on normally. A kind of artificial vertical takeoff had been achieved at last.

The implications of this feat were profound, though few, if any, experimenters recognized them at the time. Collective pitch control, by enabling the pilot to regulate lift, thrust and revolutions per minute, represented a breakthrough in helicopter design, and the mechanisms

Seen flying over Detroit in 1931, the first of 24 PCA-2 autogiros built by the Pitcairn company was used by the Detroit News to speed reporters to the scene of major stories.

A Cierva C.30 descends toward a narrow platform built over the deck of an Italian cruiser. A series of such landings and takeoffs was conducted in January 1935 by the Italian Navy to test the autogiro as a possible shipboard reconnaissance aircraft.

involved would one day be adapted to allow him to tilt the rotor itself.

Two years later, trial takeoffs were staged from the roof of the new post office in downtown Philadelphia, and the United States Department of Commerce added still more to the excitement by authorizing development of a "Roadable" autogiro that would be as much at home on the ground as in the air. In October of 1936, with Jim Ray at the controls, the little red machine landed in Washington, folded its rotors and putted through the streets on its steerable, engine-driven wheels.

In the midst of all the economic gloom, it was pleasant to dream that the autogiro would solve traffic jams and the grind of commuting, that it would speed up the mails, strengthen the national defense and reinvigorate business. Then on a foggy morning in December 1936, at London's Croydon Aerodrome, Juan de la Cierva boarded a Dutch airliner, bound for the Continent. The plane lumbered uncertainly down the runway, lifted into the air and crashed into a fog-shrouded row of buildings. The 41-year-old inventor of the autogiro was killed instantly.

The glory days of the flying windmill were fast drawing to a close, and not only because la Cierva's guiding genius was gone; economic conditions had grown so bleak that autogiro makers were unable to turn a profit. Buyers—among them Eastern Air Lines, which used the craft on some of its mail runs—could not afford the slight increase in operating costs over conventional craft. The military, which might have been expected to buy the autogiro, turned it down. The autogiro's speed, range and cargo capacity were limited and its vertical takeoff capability was dependent on a favorable head wind. So specialized a craft could not meet military requirements. But if this strange machine with whirling wings was showing signs of being an economic and technological misfit, its developers had achieved at least one signal feat. For by solving the autogiro's problems one by one, la Cierva and his colleagues had opened the way at last for the practical helicopter. 〰

Pitcairn's "Roadable" autogiro pauses for a traffic light on a Washington street. A one-of-a-kind prototype with folding rotor blades, steerable front wheels and an engine connected to both the propeller and the rear wheel, the Roadable won a Department of Commerce competition for a convertible aircraft/highway vehicle but was never commercially manufactured.

3

The dream come true

y the early 1930s, aircraft designers in several nations were once again exploring the possibilities of vertical flight. Some of them, such as Louis Breguet in France and Igor Sikorsky, who had moved to the United States in the wake of the Russian Revolution, had merely revived their long-standing interest in helicopter development. Others, such as Henrich Focke and Anton Flettner of Germany, were relative newcomers to rotary-wing aeronautical research. Working separately, all would try to untangle the complexities that still stymied the design of a true helicopter, a craft that could land and take off vertically and make a smooth transition to forward flight under the full control of its pilot.

Initially, Breguet's work seemed the most promising. Inspired perhaps by Juan de la Cierva's autogiros, he determined in 1930 to attack once more the problem of vertical flight that he had abandoned more than two decades before. He could not devote his full time to it, however; in addition to running his thriving aircraft manufacturing company, he was the head of an air transport operation and president of the old family engineering firm of Maison Breguet. He set up a new and separate concern, the Syndicate for Gyroplane Studies, and hired a young engineer named René Dorand to oversee it.

Breguet had learned caution from his earlier experiences. In 1908 he had brashly predicted success for his gyroplanes without any real understanding of the enormous mechanical and aerodynamic complexities involved. Now, he prudently named his prospective machine the *Gyroplane-Laboratoire,* clearly identifying it as a research vehicle and nothing more. To stretch the limited funds advanced by investors in his enterprise, he instructed Dorand to build the craft insofar as possible from available bits and pieces. Dorand used an old Breguet 19 airplane fuselage for the gyroplane's body and powered the machine with a surplus aircraft engine.

In November 1933, after many months of ground tests, Breguet invited his investors to watch his creation take wing. Though mechanics warned that the controls were not yet perfected, Breguet felt confident enough to schedule a brief demonstration flight. The test pilot, a young engineer and former Army pilot named Maurice Claisse, was reluctant to take the aircraft up, but rather than embarrass Breguet in front of his employer's backers, he climbed into the cockpit. With three men standing by to restrain the machine, Claisse started the engine. Above him, a

Hovering over treetops near his Connecticut headquarters, Igor Sikorsky pilots his VS-300A in April 1941. Despite its cumbersome triple tail rotors—later replaced by a single vertical rotor—the experimental craft established a national endurance record by staying aloft for more than an hour.

pair of twin-bladed rotors, nearly 54 feet long, began to turn. They rotated in opposite directions and were double-hinged to flap up and down from the root and back and forth from a midblade elbow joint.

The craft began to lift off and immediately justified the mechanics' fears. Tipping to the right despite Claisse's urgent efforts to control it, the would-be gyroplane crunched into the ground and smashed its rotors. Bystanders scrambled for safety, and Claisse escaped unhurt.

The demonstration was so dismal that Breguet might well have decided to wait several years before trying again. But the inventor persevered. Throughout 1934 and half of 1935 the machine was rebuilt, modified, ground-tested and retuned. Now, not only could Claisse control yaw, the tendency of the nose to move from side to side, by changing the pitch of the two rotors, but he could also achieve a degree of longitudinal and lateral control by tilting the whirling rotors. On June 26, 1935, Claisse made a successful lift-off, followed by several flights at speeds of 18 to 30 miles per hour. The machine seemed promising enough to attract French Air Ministry support in the form of a contract that would underwrite flight trials, with a three-million-franc bonus if all performance tests were passed.

By December, the craft was poised for its first Air Ministry demonstration at the military airfield at Villacoublay, a Paris suburb. As official observers looked on, Claisse lifted from the ground, circled a specified 547-yard course and landed safely, completing the first test. Claisse tried a week later for the second requirement—a speed of 60 miles per hour. All went well at first, but then the craft began to buck wildly and veered toward some hangars and a crowd of spectators. Claisse managed to set it down without hitting anything. However, the rotors went out of control, collided with each other and the machine was severely damaged. The Air Ministry nevertheless certified that the gyroplane had passed its speed requirement.

The craft was not repaired and ready for further tests until September 1936, when Claisse took it up to a record altitude of 518 feet. But the strain of the climb and descent buckled the metal skin of the rotors and popped some rivets. Only two days were needed for repairs; Claisse then satisfied the Air Ministry's aerial maneuver requirements, which involved banking the helicopter to the right and left in a 300-foot-wide corridor. In November, he set a helicopter endurance record of 1 hour 2 minutes 50 seconds in the air and also covered a distance of 27 miles— even though the machine developed vibrations that shook it, and him, "like a bag of walnuts." Finally, after two failed attempts to meet the hovering requirement, he maintained the craft in the air above one spot for 10 minutes. The Breguet-Dorand machine had managed to pass its tests and win the three-million-franc bonus from the Air Ministry, yet it was still a long way from being a practical helicopter.

Armed with another Air Ministry contract for further development, Breguet and Dorand continued their work but made scant progress. In June 1939 their machine was almost destroyed during an attempt at

Piloted by Major Marinello Nelli of the Regia Aeronautica, D'Ascanio's twin-rotored helicopter hovers above a cheering Roman crowd in this 1930s magazine illustration.

An Italian inventor's sweet success

In October 1930, a fragile-looking craft designed by Corradino D'Ascanio of Italy took off from an airfield near Rome, rose vertically to a height of 59 feet and flew forward for slightly more than half a mile before returning to earth eight minutes and 45 seconds later—a stunning accomplishment at the time.

The flight briefly propelled Italy to the forefront of helicopter research, establishing marks for altitude, distance and endurance that were the first ever to be recognized by the prestigious Fédération Aéronautique Internationale. And it offered the indefatigable D'Ascanio another kind of satisfaction: "When I saw my helicopter leaving the ground I was overwhelmed with emotion," the inventor recalled years later. "Not only because it was a victory—the indescribable joy of seeing many years of sacrifice and hardship now crowned by success—but particularly because I was able to prove to my children that I was not crazy."

autorotational landing. By then, a European war seemed imminent, and Breguet shelved his helicopter dream once more and turned to the full-scale production of bombers. Meanwhile, another visionary, working in Bremen, Germany, would surpass the French designer.

On June 26, 1936—exactly one year after the first lift-off of the Breguet-Dorand gyroplane—a German test pilot named Ewald Rohlfs climbed into the open cockpit of a wingless fuselage fitted with three-bladed rotors mounted on skeletal outriggers on either side. The rotors were powered by a nose-mounted 160-horsepower aircraft engine. By moving the stick forward and backward, Rohlfs could tilt the rotors forward and backward together and keep the nose from going up and down. By moving the stick sideways, he could increase the pitch, or angle, of the blades of one rotor and reduce it on the other to control roll. By using the rudder pedals, he could tilt the two rotors forward and backward in opposite directions to control yaw.

With the rotors whirling above his head, Rohlfs lifted the ungainly craft aloft and held it there for 28 seconds. Then he set it down softly on the ground. On his fourth ascent, he flew for 16 minutes.

The designer of this promising craft was Henrich Focke, a World War I pilot who had helped form the renowned Focke-Wulf aircraft company in the early 1920s. A critic of Adolf Hitler's Nazi regime, Focke had been ousted as head of the firm in 1933; he then obtained a license to build autogiros. Shortly afterward, he began to explore the possibilities of adding power to rotor blades to make a true helicopter.

Focke went about the design of his helicopter methodically, studying the work of earlier experimenters and drawing on his own experience with fixed-wing aircraft and autogiros. He refined his ideas by putting a nine-pound helicopter model through wind tunnel and flight tests and by running carefully calibrated ground trials of power-transmission systems and rotor-blade forms. The result, called the Fa-61 by Focke, was the best helicopter yet.

After conducting tentative test flights in June 1936, Focke spent many months fine-tuning his design. Then on May 10, 1937, the Fa-61 made a descent from 1,130 feet with its engine turned off and its rotors spinning, coming in for a perfect autorotational landing. By proving that his craft could use unpowered rotor support as its own built-in "parachute," just like a Cierva autogiro, Focke had done much to relieve anxiety about what would happen if a helicopter in flight were suddenly to experience engine failure. But though he had advanced helicopter design further than anyone before him, he had not anticipated the need for full collective pitch control that would allow the pilot to set smoothly all the blades at the same angle at the same time. The pilot now could put the craft into autorotation only by engaging a switch that abruptly decreased the pitch of the blades to the full autorotation position.

Seven weeks later, Focke turned Rohlfs loose to show just how effective the Fa-61 could be. In two days, Rohlfs broke every official helicop-

ter record. Some of the new marks represented only moderate improvements over those set in late 1936 by the Breguet-Dorand machine in France. Others were many times better: The Fa-61 topped the French craft's 518-foot altitude record by climbing to 7,800 feet. Equally unprecedented was the German helicopter's dependability of maneuver.

For all its astounding achievements, however, the Fa-61 made little impression on a public already familiar with airplanes and autogiros—until 25-year-old Hanna Reitsch, known throughout Germany as that nation's first woman test pilot, climbed into the cockpit. Adolf Hitler himself had recently given her the honorary rank of flight captain in recognition of her many research flights in gliders and warplanes. When she learned of Henrich Focke's marvelous new craft, she eagerly accepted an invitation to try her hand at the controls.

The propaganda value of an attractive young woman pilot did not escape the eye of Nazi officials. As soon as she had mastered the machine, she was assigned to put on a demonstration flight for Charles A. Lindbergh, who was touring Germany to assess its air power. Deeply impressed with what he witnessed, Lindbergh called Focke's helicopter the most striking aeronautical development he had ever seen.

Not long afterward, Hanna Reitsch was sent cross-country in the Fa-61, whirring across the 200 miles between Bremen and Berlin in several long hops and breaking a number of Rohlfs's records along the way. Then in February 1938 she scored her supreme publicity coup. Every night for three weeks, during performances at a trade show staged inside Berlin's cavernous Deutschlandhalle sports arena, she put on demonstrations in which she flew the helicopter vertically, backward, forward and sideways. Despite unpredictable eddies of turbulent air stirred up by the rotors' downwash, Hanna Reitsch's mastery of the machine made it look totally safe to the audiences that packed the seats.

Newsreels and photographs of the Fa-61's performance would appear around the world, and the helicopter's future seemed assured. The

Nazis softened their attitude toward Focke, and in 1937 he and the aerobatic pilot Gerd Achgelis were allowed to form a new helicopter company. Not long after Hanna Reitsch's flights in Berlin, the government awarded Focke-Achgelis a contract for an enlarged version of the Fa-61 that could lift an unprecedented 1,500 pounds of useful load.

Spurred by the outbreak of war in September 1939, Focke had his new machine, designated the Fa-223, ready for flight testing by the spring of 1940. The powerful craft had a 1,000-horsepower engine to turn the two triple-bladed 39-foot rotors mounted on its outriggers and was more than 80 feet wide and 40 feet long. Instead of the nose prop and open cockpit of the Fa-61, the Fa-223 had a four-seat cabin covered by a greenhouse-style canopy that stretched forward all the way to the monster's snout, giving the *Drache* (the dragon), as it was called, a surprisingly modern appearance. Eight farm-machine seats could be fastened outside, where additional passengers could sit if speeds were held low. Three prototypes were built; they proved able to fly at 115 miles per hour, rise to 23,400 feet with a light load and—at lower speeds and altitudes—transport loads weighing a full ton slung on 30- to 50-foot cables dangling beneath the craft.

But Focke was not the only German who was making progress in helicopter design. Indeed, he had been overtaken in several important aspects by Anton Flettner, whose career as an inventive aeronautical scientist dated back to 1905 and his experiments with remote-control devices for dirigibles. He later took up the study of vertical flight and in 1930 built his first helicopter, a bizarre craft with two small engines and propellers attached directly to the blades of the main lifting rotor. Flettner, a systematic and practical engineer, saw that the design's mechanical and aerodynamic complexities would keep his helicopter from ever becoming a practical flying machine. When it was destroyed by a sudden gust during tethered testing in 1933, he went back to basics and built an autogiro, the Fl-184, to learn more about control mechanisms. The Fl-184 had full cyclic control—that is, the pilot could tilt the rotor by moving the control stick in the direction he wished the craft to fly.

Encouraged by the Fl-184's success as an autogiro, Flettner added power to the lifting rotor and devised a collective pitch control similar to the one already developed by la Cierva but with a different purpose. It allowed the pilot to vary the pitch of all the blades of the lifting rotor freely and simultaneously, permitting a smooth shift from powered flight to autorotation. Flettner removed the main propeller at the nose and replaced it with two smaller props on outriggers to the side, partly for thrust and partly to counter torque.

Flettner's design was complicated, but it was based on a solid understanding of the aerodynamic forces involved. It was hardly elegant, but the helicopter worked. By feeding power to the main rotor and shifting one of the outrigger propellers into reverse to counter torque, the pilot could get the machine to hover. By removing power from the main rotor and using both outrigger pro-

Test pilot Hanna Reitsch confers with designer Henrich Focke before her 1938 exhibition flight of his twin-rotored Fa-61 at a trade show held inside a Berlin sports arena. Below, at left, she hovers above a throng. For safety, the arena was aired periodically: The crowd consumed enough oxygen to reduce the engine's power.

pellers to provide thrust, he could convert the craft into an autogiro.

In 1937 Flettner used his recently acquired knowledge to come up with a strikingly original concept in the Fl-265, a true helicopter that had two counter-rotating rotors driven by a common gearbox. These were set close together on separate shafts and were splayed outward and away from each other so that they intermeshed like the blades of an egg beater. The German Navy was impressed enough to award a small production contract to Flettner in 1938. The Fl-265 made its first flight in May of 1939 and by August had shown that it was fully controllable and could move in and out of autorotation freely. An improved version, the Fl-282 *Kolibri,* or hummingbird, appeared in 1940. Much smaller and five times lighter than Focke's Fa-223, the *Kolibri* could fly at almost 90 miles per hour, climb to 13,000 feet, and carry 800 pounds of fuel, crew and useful load.

The craft also showed considerable military promise, particularly as a submarine spotter. In early 1941, seeking to determine how the *Kolibri* might fare at the hands of enemy fighter planes, the German Navy used a pair of fighters equipped with gun cameras and staged a 20 minute mock attack on one of Flettner's helicopters. The film showed that neither fighter pilot had been able to get the nimble *Kolibri* in his sights. Other tests demonstrated that the craft could take off from and land on the gun turret of a cruiser even in heavy seas.

Henrich Focke continued to make progress with his enormous Fa-223, but it was now clear that the little *Kolibri* had become the world's first helicopter to be developed to a practical stage, able to do useful work and ready for wartime deployment. Naval authorities, confident that the helicopter had a part to play in the growing conflict, placed a mass-production order for 1,000 of the craft.

German achievements were not lost on Igor Sikorsky in the United States; in fact, they were among the goads that spurred him to work on the design of a craft that would incorporate an ingenious feature and make the helicopter a truly viable machine.

After abandoning his earlier helicopter studies in 1910, Sikorsky had gone on to win renown as Russia's foremost aircraft designer of World War I. When the Bolsheviks took over, however, he chose to seek his fortune elsewhere. After living briefly in Paris, he moved in 1919 to the United States, where he worked for a time on an Army trimotor bomber project. Then, having been told that aviation was a "dying industry" by a gloomy colonel who saw the postwar era as one only of surplus aircraft and unemployed fliers, Sikorsky settled in for a jobless year in New York, living in progressively smaller quarters and subsisting largely on a diet of beans, bread and coffee.

Sikorsky finally landed a job teaching mathematics at a night school for Russian immigrants, supplementing his teacher's pay by lecturing on developments in aviation. In the spring of 1923 he and a few of his supporters scraped together some financing and established the Sikor-

An elderly Henrich Focke displays a model of the sturdy Fa-223 helicopter he produced for Germany during World War II. At the end of the War, an Fa-223 captured by the British made the first helicopter flight across the English Channel.

Anton Flettner, designer of the Kolibri, or hummingbird, a craft with intermeshing rotors, stands proudly before a fleet of his helicopters at the plant near Berlin in 1943. The pilot sat in front of the engine, in the open—which provided a clear view for military observation and submarine spotting.

sky Aero Engineering Corporation on a Long Island chicken farm owned by a fellow Russian émigré. There, in a cluster of ramshackle buildings, Sikorsky and a handful of employees began building his S-29A, an all-metal, twin-engined transport. The A stood for American—"I was sufficiently grateful to my newly adopted country to put in the A," he wrote later. On its initial test flight, the S-29 crash-landed, but after repairs, made it up into the air and down again without incident and proved, as Sikorsky proudly noted, "a very strong machine." Indeed, the S-29 went on to a long career as a transport, standing up to "hard service, rough landings, bad weather and continuous work."

Over the next few years, Sikorsky produced nine planes of various types, but not until 1928, when his S-38 amphibian won wide acclaim, did orders begin pouring in. The public imagination had been stirred by Lindbergh's flight across the Atlantic the year before, and a passenger-carrying amphibian, long a dream of Sikorsky's, now seemed the way to put Europe and the other continents within convenient grasp of the many. He would ultimately sell 114 of the eight-passenger S-38s, and by 1929 he would be creating a far bigger 40-passenger flying boat for Pan American Airways. Also in 1929, Sikorsky renamed his company the Sikorsky Aviation Corporation and moved its operations to Stratford, Connecticut, near Bridgeport, where it soon became a

Wearing the fedora that would become his trademark, Igor Sikorsky stands on lower Broadway shortly after his arrival in New York from Russia in 1919. "I found what I had hoped for," Sikorsky said later, "a dynamic, forceful, progressive country."

subsidiary of the giant United Aircraft and Transport Corporation.

Freed from the pressing financial problems that face a small enterprise, Sikorsky could now revive his old interest in helicopters. At home and in stolen moments at the plant, he pored over every published report of rotary-winged attempts, studied the improved engines and lighter materials becoming available, and pondered the Cierva autogiro's proof that autorotation might enable a helicopter to survive engine failure. He made detailed sketches of possible helicopter designs. These ranged from a streamlined, single-main-rotor craft to an imaginative adaptation of the S-38 amphibian in which a turbine engine buried in the hull would power the rotor as well as the two standard props.

Then in late 1930 he wrote a prophetic memo to the management of United Aircraft, stating that a helicopter that could land on top of buildings, on ships and in tiny parks could be built. He urged the company to develop "in a reasonable and economical way our own type of helicopter." But the Wall Street collapse of October 1929 and the onset of the Depression meant that financial support for such marginal-sounding projects was out of the question. In any case, airplane projects continued to occupy much of Sikorsky's time, and in 1931 his 40-passenger S-40, christened the *American Clipper,* was ready to fly. It made its first flight, with Lindbergh at the controls, from Miami to the Panama Canal, stopping in Cuba and Jamaica. The S-40 was the beginning of a revolution in flying boats and would be followed by the S-41 with a 1,500-mile range and the ocean-hopping S-42 with a 3,000-mile range.

Busy as they were designing and building amphibians, Sikorsky and a few key aides kept working on the helicopter problem. Sometimes it was even possible for them to sneak an unauthorized rotary-wing experiment into the company wind tunnel. In mid-1931, Sikorsky quietly applied for a patent (he would receive it in 1935) on the most basic helicopter configuration of all: a single lifting rotor with a small vertical rotor on the tail to counteract torque.

Unfortunately for Sikorsky, the advancing Depression and competition from other plane makers kept his subsidiary from making a penny. Finally, in late 1938, a senior official of United Aircraft summoned the celebrated designer to his office to inform him that all production at the faltering Sikorsky division was to be shut down. The executive did offer one ray of hope: The company, he said, would seriously consider any personal research project that Sikorsky might want to work on, as long as it was not too costly. The designer had an immediate proposal. He would build a research helicopter, and he pleaded with the company to keep his crack engineering team intact to assist him with the project.

Given the go-ahead, Sikorsky was well prepared for a fast start. An avid follower of other rotorcraft efforts, he had observed autogiros leaping off the roof of Philadelphia's post office and had gone to Germany to see Focke's Fa-61 in action. (In March 1939 he would travel to France to watch Maurice Claisse demonstrate Breguet's experimental gyroplane.) The simplest approach might be to adopt the basic format of one or the other of the first two successful helicopters, designed by Breguet and by Focke—the French coaxial, counter-rotating configuration, or the German side-by-side outrigger rotors. But Sikorsky's instincts told him that the most efficient layout was the one he had already patented, which relied on a single main rotor plus a small vertical tail rotor.

Mindful of the corporate dictum to watch the budget, Sikorsky tried out various tail rotors on a makeshift test stand put together from metal pipes and a 25-horsepower motorcycle engine hooked up to the differential gears from an old Dodge automobile. He finally settled on a two-bladed rotor about three feet long, and during the spring of 1939 the design was firmed up and blueprints were drawn.

On September 14—just two weeks after the outbreak of war in Europe—Sikorsky's creation was rolled out on its four wheels into the yard next to the factory. Called the VS-300, it was a mere skeleton of metal tubes, with an open perch for the pilot in front of the 75-horsepower engine. A flimsy-looking system of pulleys and V-belts, plus the heavy-duty gears from a truck transmission, transferred the engine's power to the single main rotor, whose three blades described a circle 28 feet in diameter. A skinny tail boom jutted rearward to hold the two-bladed antitorque rotor.

For its first trial, with Igor Sikorsky himself at the controls, the VS-300 was tethered to a tray of heavy weights on the ground. After climbing onto the pilot's perch, Sikorsky revved the engine carefully, and the delicate contraption began to sway back and forth and vibrate all over. To the few observers, the designer-pilot began to look like a blur. But Sikorsky could feel the machine try to rise. He pulled up on the collective pitch control lever, so that the blades would bite more air, and all four wheels unmistakably lifted off the ground. Sikorsky immediately decreased the pitch and let the VS-300 settle back down. Before quitting for the day he rose from the ground several more times, totaling an estimated 10 seconds of precarious, vibration-racked hops.

The shaky start proved the wisdom of employing an uncovered, skeletal framework, since even radical design changes could be made overnight. Tubes, struts and sheet metal could easily be added, subtracted or moved to new positions, and transmission ratios could be quickly modified by tinkering with the pulley-belt system. Sikorsky began the first of many alterations to damp down the vibrations and balance the flight controls. It was a hit-or-miss process, and the frustrations were many. "The only thing we knew was that we had very little reliable information about helicopters," he explained later, "and no flight experience whatsoever."

Sikorsky and one or two aides continued to practice piloting techniques in a flight simulator suspended in the hangar, and in brief flights outside. Sometimes, the untrustworthy craft would drag its tethering weights across the ground and even lift free. The mechanics, never knowing what overnight modification they might have to perform next, came to refer to the machine as "Igor's nightmare." But as the pilots' flight time built up and refinements of the mechanism continued, control seemed a little better and the weights gave way to a ball-and-chain anchor that let the VS-300 rise several feet. By November 1939, the craft was making hops that lasted a minute or two. Then in December, a gust of wind toppled the unstable machine, smashing the rotor blades.

Sikorsky decided to make a major change in the control system. Leaving the vertical antitorque rotor in its place at the tail, he installed a sizable pair of rear-mounted outriggers and topped each with a horizontal rotor. In this new control scheme, the vertical rotor would continue to neutralize torque, while the horizontal rotors, working together, would raise or lower the tail, which, in turn, would tilt the main rotor and make the helicopter move forward or backward. Working individually, the new rotors would roll the craft to one side or the other. Thus, all direc-

tional control except that for straight up and down was handled by the ungainly tail, eliminating the need for a cyclic pitch in the main rotor hub. All the main rotor had to do was provide upward lift or angled thrust whenever the entire craft was tilted in any direction.

Cautious flight tests of the redesigned VS-300 began early in 1940. The craft was clearly more stable and tethers gave way to men holding ropes while the pilot learned to control the machine. Finally it seemed safe to forgo these, too, and on May 13, 1940, Sikorsky—who had done much of the preliminary testing himself—took the pilot's perch and lifted the VS-300 in its first truly free flight. A week later Sikorsky demonstrated his machine to a select group of guests. Seemingly in complete command of his odd vehicle, he flew straight up and down, went sideways and backwards, rotated and hovered above a fixed spot. Nobody remarked on the fact that the craft did not fly forward.

By now, Sikorsky had some American competition. At about the same time that Sikorsky was putting his VS-300 through its still-limited paces, the Army Air Corps was negotiating a contract with another helicopter designer, W. Laurence LePage. An engineer who had once worked for the Pitcairn autogiro concern outside Philadelphia, LePage had been deeply impressed by the performance of Henrich Focke's twin-rotored Fa-61; recently, he had teamed up with New York engineer-inventor Havilland H. Platt to form the Platt-LePage Aircraft Company, intending to build a helicopter modeled after

Going for a ride, Sikorsky sits bundled up at the controls of his VS-300. During the early years of its development, the designer insisted on serving as test pilot. "I must take the blame for our occasional flight trouble," he explained, "if I am to accept any of the credit for the helicopter's success later."

the Focke machine. The Air Corps, mindful that the United States might need such craft in the event of American involvement in the European war, awarded Platt-LePage a $300,000 contract to develop an XR-1—experimental rotary-winged aircraft No. 1.

During the early summer of 1940, Sikorsky continued to stage public demonstrations of his VS-300, even as he made adjustments to remedy its deficiencies. "I had never been in a machine that was as pleasant to fly as this light helicopter was, with a completely open cockpit," he wrote later. "It was like a dream to feel the machine lift you gently up in the air, float smoothly over one spot, move up or down, and move not only forward or backward but in any direction."

The craft could now remain aloft for 15 minutes, and movies of the flights showed it hovering close enough to a man standing on some rocks for him to place a suitcase in a wire basket fixed to the VS-300's nose and then take it out again. But while reviewing these movies, a United Aircraft executive—the same one who had announced the demise of the Sikorsky flying boat enterprise—noticed that the VS-300 flew in every direction but straight ahead. He asked Sikorsky about this shortcoming, and the ever-resourceful designer replied: "That is one of the minor engineering problems that we haven't yet solved." It was, in fact, not so minor: Sikorsky had chosen not to show the craft in forward flight because turbulent air from the main rotor, buffeting the horizontal tail rotors, could cause the helicopter to vibrate.

This problem—along with others—had to be solved. Through further tests Sikorsky and his assistants collected enough engineering data to make improvements. Among other things, they added oil dampeners that reduced vibration, and the helicopter performed somewhat better in forward flight. To give it greater lifting power, they installed a new engine. Now, the VS-300 could fly at 30 to 40 miles per hour.

Meanwhile, the Air Corps, in spite of its commitment to the Platt-LePage XR-1, was still casting about for other likely designs. And in July 1940, an important military visitor arrived at Stratford to test-fly the VS-300. Captain Hollingsworth Franklin "Frank" Gregory, project officer for the budding United States helicopter program, was a seasoned autogiro pilot, and after a few instructions from Sikorsky he lifted gingerly from the ground. Following some uneventful maneuvers, Gregory began to fly forward, but the wayward VS-300—which had behaved with Sikorsky at the controls—soon started to bob erratically through the air; at the same time, it seemed determined to climb unstoppably. With great skill—and a bit of luck—Gregory finally managed to set the craft down safely on the ground.

"More than anything else," Gregory wrote later, "VS-300 reminded me of a bucking bronco. She was ornery. When I wanted her to go down she went up. When I tried to back her up she persisted on going forward. About the only thing she was agreeable to was getting down again and that probably was because she wanted to get fed and pampered by the mechanics and her maker." Sikorsky knew what had gone wrong: After the helicopter moved from a hover into forward flight, it experienced a sudden burst of surplus power, causing it to shoot up in the air. Once he had explained the problem to Gregory and given him a few more pointers, the pilot tried again, but not before showing his confidence in his ability to master the new craft. He placed a weighted handkerchief by the nose skid as a marker, and after putting the VS-300 through its paces, he returned for a precise landing at the same spot.

Impressed by the VS-300, Gregory recommended that the Army back a Sikorsky military helicopter, regardless of the commitment to sponsor the Platt-LePage machine. On December 17, 1940, a panel of government officials met to evaluate Gregory's report, view some movies of the VS-300 in action and make a final decision. They agreed that $50,000 of partial support should be squeezed out to help Sikorsky build an experimental helicopter for the Army Air Corps. Specifications called for a closed-cabin two-seater twice as big and powerful as the VS-300. It would be designated the XR-4—XR-2 and XR-3 were modified autogiros built by the Kellett Autogiro Corporation.

Sikorsky moved quickly to design and build the XR-4. At the same time, he redoubled his efforts to iron out the vibration problems and devise a satisfactory control system for the VS-300, which was still flying with the three-rotor tail. Once, a tail outrigger gave way and Sikorsky crashed from 20 feet up. Unhurt and undaunted, he continued to modi-

Hovering so low and so steadily that an assistant can place a parcel in a basket attached to the craft's nose, Sikorsky demonstrates the maneuverability of his completed VS-300. Pontoons beneath the helicopter allowed it to be operated from both land and water.

fy his design, and on May 6, 1941, he invited a committee of official witnesses to watch him try to break the world's helicopter endurance record set by Focke's Fa-61 in 1937. (After 1938, the Germans had concealed the performance levels of their helicopters behind a curtain of military censorship.) To the press in attendance he drolly said, "You will witness the most unspectacular event you have ever covered. I plan only to hang stationary over one spot for about an hour and a half, and nothing more." Barely able to leave the ground with nearly 15 gallons of gasoline—28 pounds more load than ever before—Sikorsky gently lifted off several feet and fulfilled his promise, hovering 12 minutes beyond the best of the old Fa-61 marks. Even so, the continuing awkwardness of the triple tail control, especially in forward flight, made it obvious that more modifications and test flights in the VS-300 were needed before Sikorsky could arrive at a final design for the Army XR-4.

To Sikorsky's chagrin, the rival Platt-LePage project seemed to be right on schedule. More than twice the size of Sikorsky's proposed XR-4, the XR-1 made its first tethered lift-off six days after the VS-300 had set its endurance record. Less than a week later, the Platt-LePage craft made several untethered flights, rising about three feet off the ground but never staying up longer than half a minute. Its builders and the Air Corps realized that major engineering refinements still had to be made before the XR-1 would be controllable for higher and longer test flights.

Eager to get on with the XR-4, Sikorsky called on his engineering team in June 1941 to try something new on the VS-300. The two clumsy outriggers holding the horizontal tail rotors were cut off and replaced with a single horizontal prop mounted on a little pylon added to the tail boom. The change worked wonders; the craft was much more controllable, and was soon flying stably forward at 70 miles per hour. But Sikorsky was convinced that still further simplification could be achieved: All control would be put back into the main rotor, using cyclic pitch changes. Only the single vertical prop on the tail would be needed to counteract torque. He had, on his own, duplicated Anton Flettner's conclusion; cyclic pitch controls were the solution to the problem of controlling a helicopter's longitudinal and lateral movements. In appearance the VS-300 was still much as it had been at the outset, but so many other modifications and improvements had been made during the past three years that Sikorsky believed the craft would now perform as a true vertical-flight machine.

On December 8, 1941—the day after the Japanese attack on Pearl Harbor—the VS-300 was first flown in its final configuration. By New Year's Eve it was flying in all directions and handling better than ever. Meanwhile, the much larger Sikorsky XR-4 was being fitted with the same control scheme, and on January 14, 1942, the new helicopter was wheeled out of its hangar for a trial flight.

Four men hung on to the landing gear to prevent a premature lift-off as test pilot Charles Lester Morris checked out the engine and controls.

Ready at last, Morris opened the throttle, raised the collective pitch lever and lifted off the ground. As Sikorsky stood below and waved, Morris stayed in the air for three minutes and then set down for some adjustments. The second time up, he remained aloft for a little more than five minutes before quitting for lunch. By the end of the day, Morris had made four more flights, logging 25 minutes of air time in the XR-4.

Sikorsky and his engineers continued to refine the XR-4's design, and by May the craft was ready for delivery to the Army at Wright Field, in Dayton, Ohio. Les Morris flew the finished helicopter to its destination in 16 careful hops, taking five days but spending little more than 16 hours in the air. With Sikorsky beside him in the enclosed cabin, he would hover and check the route by reading highway signs or by asking information of a startled motorist. On one occasion he deliberately overshot the landing site and flew on for 100 feet. Then he slowly backed the helicopter to the spot and gently landed it. According to Sikorsky, one of the airport mechanics who had been watching from the ground remarked, "I don't know whether I'm crazy or drunk." Sikorsky and Morris touched down at Wright Field on May 17. The next day Orville Wright was among those who came to congratulate them.

In December, after running the new craft through extensive shakedown flights, the Army contracted for production to begin and also placed an order for a new, larger model. Four months later, in April 1943, it requested still another version. Sikorsky was clearly taking the worldwide lead in helicopter design and manufacturing. The Platt-LePage experimental model was not performing well enough to warrant a production contract, and in Germany, Allied bombing raids were disrupting the planned production of Henrich Focke's Fa-223 and Anton Flettner's nimble *Kolibri*—though Flettner's machines saw limited service during World War II.

More than 400 Sikorsky helicopters would roll off the assembly lines by the end of the War. The novel craft would not alter the course of the conflict. Helicopters were still too limited in their capabilities. They lacked speed; they could carry only small loads, and when used at sea, they had difficulty operating from the windswept, pitching decks of warships. But then, in April 1944, Lieutenant Carter Harman of the U.S. Army Air Forces flew into the steamy jungles of northern Burma and proved that the helicopter had a definite military role to perform.

Harman, piloting a Sikorsky YR-4 (the X for experimental was replaced by a Y for a service-test model), had been summoned from his base in India to a secret outpost behind Japanese lines in the Burmese jungle. There, American forces were supporting British raiders who were seeking to reopen the Burma Road, a vital supply link between Allied forces in India and China. After following a circuitous 600-mile route to his destination, Harman received his orders: He was to pluck a stranded American pilot and three British casualties from the jungle 30 miles to the south. The pilot, flying a tiny L-1 liaison plane, had been bringing the Englishmen out when engine trouble forced him down.

Orville Wright and Colonel Frank Gregory, rotary-wing project officer for the Army, congratulate Sikorsky on delivery of the first helicopter to the Army, in 1942. During the odd new craft's cross-country flight to an Ohio base, an alarmed air-raid spotter described it as a flying windmill.

With no suitable landing strip nearby, the four men seemed doomed.

After watching Harman whirl down out of the sky for a vertical landing in a nearby paddy, the American L-1 pilot said to him: "You look like an angel!" But the angel faced a problem. The altitude, humidity and heat had thinned the air, sharply reducing the engine's power and the rotor blades' lifting capacity. Harman knew that the YR-4 could barely hover with only himself on board. His single hope was to jump abruptly aloft, then ease quickly into forward flight (one of the peculiarities of helicopters is that they need much more power to hover than to fly forward at moderate speeds), taking the men out one at a time.

With one of the injured Englishmen beside him in the cabin, Harman gunned the engine, revving his rotor to the limit, and pulled up on the collective pitch lever; the straining copter jumped nearly 20 feet above the paddy, quickly dissipating the stored-up kinetic energy in its rotor blades. Then Harman nosed forward to pick up forward speed and vaulted over some nearby trees. About 10 miles away, he unloaded his passenger in a dried-out riverbed from which L-5s could operate, then went back for the next rescue. After the second trip out, his engine became so dangerously overheated that he had to stop for the day, but he returned the next morning for two more lifts.

Harman performed several more such jungle rescues before returning to India two weeks later. The helicopter had shown that it could be a truly useful aircraft, a rotary-winged angel of mercy. In the years to come it would be that and more, in peace as well as war. ～

A pioneering rescue mission

In the closing months of World War II, the virtually impenetrable jungles of Southeast Asia provided a rigorous testing ground for the capabilities of the newly operational Sikorsky R-4 as a rescue vehicle. There, where dense foliage, precipitous terrain and the presence of the enemy often prevented the overland evacuation of the wounded, the ability of a helicopter to land and take off from a small clearing or a narrow riverbed meant the difference between life and death for many an Allied soldier.

In the unusually well-documented rescue depicted on these pages, a pilot, Captain James Green of the U.S. Tenth Air Force, had crashed just three minutes' flying time from Shinbwiyang Air Field in northern Burma, but he was too badly injured to be carried back to base. In fact, once his plane was spotted from the air, it took rescue and medical teams a day and a half to reach him.

A helicopter was the only answer. However, the territory for miles around the crash site was so hilly and thickly forested that there was no spot for one to touch down. For two weeks, a detachment of combat engineers, a special Air Transport Command rescue crew and a group of Tenth Air Force volunteers labored to clear and level a nearby hilltop, using supplies and equipment dropped by air. When the landing area was ready, the rescue itself went so smoothly as to be almost anticlimactic. A Sikorsky R-4 picked up Captain Green early on the morning of April 4 and delivered him minutes later to the hospital at Shinbwiyang Air Field.

A downed PT-19 is partially hidden among the palm trees on a Burmese hillside. The parachute visible just downhill from the plane served as a shelter for the injured pilot. The two others belong to radio operators who were dropped to guide rescue parties and administer first aid.

Before the pilot can be evacuated, volunteers from the nearby airfield work to clear a helicopter landing space in the dense jungle. On a selected hilltop, trees are felled, cut into movable pieces with a chain saw (top left) and hauled away; the hilltop is then leveled with explosives and man-powered earthmovers (center left), and finally the landing area is smoothed with a heavy log "grader" (bottom left).

A team of rescuers carries the pilot to the clearing just before daybreak to await the arrival of the helicopter.

The rescue helicopter is ready to receive its passenger on the dusty landing area. A parachute set up at the edge of the clearing shields the injured man from the tropical sun.

With the injured man safely aboard, the
R-4 lifts off from the jungle clearing, bound
for Shinbwiyang Air Field.

At Shinbwiyang, the rescued pilot is carefully
taken from the helicopter and put on a
stretcher for the trip to the base hospital.

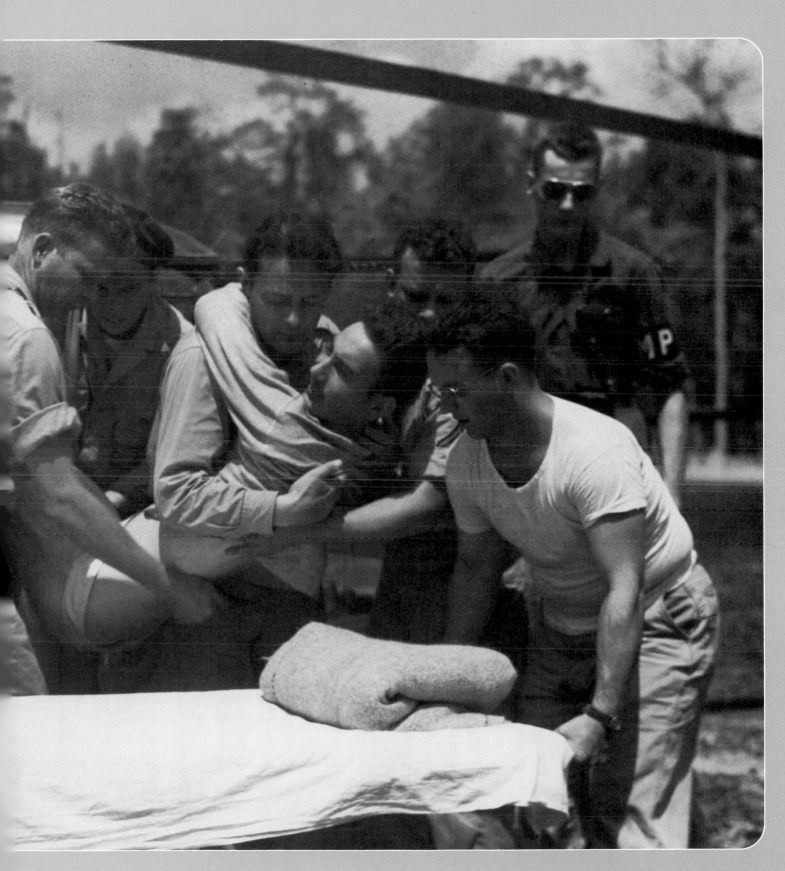

FOCKE-ACHGELIS FA-61 (1936)
The Fa-61 is generally regarded as the world's first unequivocally successful helicopter. Its propeller was intentionally made too small to pull the machine forward; the propeller served to cool the engine with a steady flow of air.

FLETTNER FL-282 *KOLIBRI* (1940)
Though substantially smaller and lighter than the Fa-61, the German Kolibri (hummingbird) could carry three times as many people. Besides a cockpit for the pilot and copilot in front of the rotors, there was an observer's compartment behind them with a single seat facing the rear.

Helicopters of the piston era

In pursuit of their goal—a functional helicopter that would fly under perfect control—the pioneer designers arrived at a number of solutions that set their machines widely apart. And yet in spite of the dazzling variety of aircraft, early generations of helicopters shared a common feature: All were powered by air-cooled reciprocating engines instead of the liquid-cooled type. The major advantage was that air-cooled power plants did not need radiators to keep them from overheating. This saved weight and, when it came to military uses for the helicopter, the absence of coolant pipes and radiators made air-cooled engines simpler to repair in the field and less vulnerable to fire from small-caliber weapons.

The piston-engined helicopters shown in this essay represent milestones in the state of the art. Beginning with the German Fa-61 in 1936, and continuing through the American H-21 in 1952, the power of the piston helicopter's engines increased more than sevenfold, carrying capacity expanded from a lone pilot to a crew and passengers numbering up to 16, and the altitude at which the craft could fly soared from less than 8,000 feet to 17,000 feet.

The designations used here for each model are the most common ones; they varied from country to country and in the U.S. military from one service to another. (Sikorsky called its famed Korean War helicopter the S-55, while the U.S. Army designated it the H-19, the Navy the HO4S-1 and the Marines the HRS-1.) Dates in parentheses signify when the model first appeared, although the military markings or the livery that the craft wears may be of a later period. Helicopters on facing pages are presented in scale.

SIKORSKY VS-300 (1942)

A single main rotor and vertical tail rotor to control torque set the single-seat VS-300 apart from earlier helicopters, which had counter-rotating main rotors to neutralize torque. Wires from the main-rotor hub kept the hinged blades from drooping. A pennant fixed to the nose told the pilot whether he was flying the craft correctly: If the pennant was not pointing directly at him, he was sliding sideways through the air, wasting fuel and sacrificing speed.

SIKORSKY R-4 (1943)

An exhaust pipe from the enclosed engine curves up one side of the R-4, which is seen here wearing U.S. Army Air Forces colors for World War II service in Burma. Of the 185 horsepower available from the engine, about 170 was needed to lift the R-4 and its 530-pound payload; the remainder turned the tail rotor. Top speed was about 75 mph, and maximum altitude was 8,000 feet.

BELL 47G (1949)

The Bell three-seater, with its bug-eyed canopy, skeletal tail and exposed engine, won fame both as a military workhorse and a versatile commercial helicopter. By the

time production finally ended in 1973, more than 3,000 47Gs in 13 versions had been sold in more than 40 countries, for uses ranging from rescue work to crop-dusting.

PIASECKI H-21 (1952)

This tandem-rotor H-21, bearing the tricolor roundel of France, has two vertical stabilizers to help the pilot hold the craft on a straight course. The engine, positioned in the tail section behind the rear landing gear, balances the load in the cabin.

SIKORSKY S-55 (1945)

By placing the engine in the nose of the S-55, a helicopter widely used in Korea, Sikorsky gained room for a 10-passenger cabin. The engine was linked to the rotor by a slanted drive shaft that passed between the seats in the cockpit. The craft shown here wears the colors of the Royal Canadian Navy, which used the S-55 for rescue work.

4

The chopper comes of age

On November 29, 1945, a violent storm whipped across Long Island Sound and drove an oil barge aground on a reef a quarter of a mile off the Connecticut coast. Churning seas continued through the night, keeping rescue boats from the scene and threatening to pound the stricken vessel to pieces. Lashed by rain and winds of up to 60 miles per hour, the two crewmen on board had nearly given up hope when they heard an unfamiliar sound in the distance, then saw a strange wingless aircraft approaching them.

Piloting the craft, an Army R-5 helicopter flown through the storm from the Sikorsky factory in nearby Bridgeport, was Dimitri D. "Jimmy" Viner, Igor Sikorsky's nephew. Behind him in the cramped cabin was Army Captain Jackson E. Beighle, ready to man a winch-powered rescue hoist. The hoist had been developed and tested during the War by Commander Frank Erickson of the United States Coast Guard, but this would be one of its first uses in peacetime, and the first time that a helicopter had tried to pluck men from a sinking vessel.

Viner, one of the nation's most seasoned helicopter pilots, deftly maneuvered the R-5 into a hover above the battered barge. As he struggled to hold the craft in the howling wind, Beighle lowered his hoist and winched one of the stranded seamen up to safety. Viner took his bedraggled passenger to shore and returned to retrieve the remaining man. But this time the winch jammed before Beighle could reel the sailor aboard. Undismayed, Viner flew back to land with the man dangling from the hoist, and set him gently on the ground.

To helicopter enthusiasts, Jimmy Viner's dramatic rescue mission was merely a foretaste of the helicopter's boundless future. Sikorsky had predicted in 1942 that in the future hundreds of thousands of helicopters would be produced and that in such numbers the craft would sell for little more than an automobile. It seemed possible that every American would one day have a rotary-winged craft in the driveway; this had been Harold Pitcairn's dream for his autogiro in the 1930s, but the essential technology did not exist at that time. Now it did, and by 1947 more than 70 companies were working at helicopter development. Government agencies were deluged with inquiries about setting up short-haul helicopter passenger service; even the Greyhound bus company filed an application to start intercity copter runs.

Unfortunately for the dreamers, only a handful of the nation's helicopter designers were building aircraft of any real promise. Among the

Ready for battle, U.S. Marines in Korea dash from a Sikorsky HRS-1 during the first large-scale transport of troops by helicopter, in 1951. Only 12 choppers flying in relays were needed to lift 1,000 men and their equipment to the front; bringing them in by truck would have required 175 vehicles.

most original was one by Frank Piasecki, featuring tandem rotors mounted at the front and rear of an elongated fuselage. This arrangement was similar to the configuration Frenchman Paul Cornu had used in his historic vehicle of 1907, but other experimenters had not tried it since, concentrating instead on single-rotor systems mounted a bit forward of amidships.

Piasecki, the son of an immigrant Polish tailor, had rushed headlong into his career in aviation. Born in Philadelphia in 1919, he had worked while still in his teens for the Kellett Aircraft Corporation, an autogiro manufacturer. By the time he was 20, he had earned a degree in mechanical engineering from the University of Pennsylvania and an aeronautical engineering degree from New York University; he then served as a designer for the Platt-LePage Aircraft Company, which was, at the time, in competition with Sikorsky for the development of an Army helicopter.

In 1940 the enterprising Piasecki, exempted from military service during World War II because of his critically needed skills as an aeronautical engineer, gained the support of a few friends and started his own company on the side. Working out of a garage in Philadelphia, he built a Sikorsky-style helicopter with a single main rotor; by the spring of 1943 he was test-flying the machine around the countryside, and he once startled a filling station attendant by setting down for a tank of fuel and a windshield wipe.

In the meantime, Piasecki had been making progress with his tandem-rotor concept for a heavy-duty transport helicopter. The craft's load would be spread between two rotors, each of which would be smaller and simpler to build than a single rotor of the same lifting capacity. And by using them to support the helicopter at both ends, he ensured that cargo could be loaded almost haphazardly in the fuselage without dangerously affecting the balance of the craft. Designated the PV-3, the new helicopter made its first flight in March 1945.

Piasecki pressed for military support of his radical tandem-rotor idea. He at last managed to get a Navy contract and shortly after the War was delivering his odd-looking helicopter to the Navy, Marines and Coast Guard. Because the craft curved upward at the ends to keep the rotors from interfering with each other, it soon acquired the nickname Flying Banana. For a while at least, it had the distinction of being the world's largest helicopter, and could carry 12 men, including the pilot and copilot. The PV-3, only 22 of which were built, established the practicality of the tandem-rotor helicopter. Over the next two decades, it would evolve into a variety of capable multipurpose craft produced by the hundreds.

Another successful helicopter designer of the day was Arthur Young. The scion of a wealthy family, Young had been considered something of an eccentric in his hometown of Drifton, Pennsylvania. After his graduation from Princeton University in 1927, he spent most of his time experimenting with model helicopters and even hired a young

Demonstrating a troop-rescue technique in 1948, men ascend a rope ladder to a hovering HRP-1, designed by Frank Piasecki (inset).

assistant, Bartram Kelley, to help him. Just a month before the Japanese attack on Pearl Harbor, Young persuaded the Bell Aircraft Corporation of Buffalo, New York, to sponsor him in the development of a full-sized helicopter called the Model 30. It made its first untethered flight in June 1943.

At first glance, the machine looked like another Sikorsky, with a single main rotor and a small stabilizing propeller on the tail. The Model 30, however, had a simplified rotor with just two blades. A second Model 30 prototype proved itself when it was flown to the rescue of two men stranded on a crumbling ice floe in Lake Erie. Then in the following December, yet a third version of the Model 30 took to the air. Redesignated the Model 47, it was soon rolling off the Bell production lines, and in March 1946 it became the first helicopter to win Civil Aeronautics Administration certification for commercial use. Readily recognized by its two-seat, bulbous plastic cockpit and the characteristic "clop-clop-clop" sound (hence the term "chopper") of its twin-bladed rotor, the Model 47 was to set a helicopter industry record by remaining in production for three decades.

Stanley Hiller, a young dropout from the University of California, would advance helicopter design still further. Hiller was only 19 when he built and flew a coaxial, double-rotor helicopter in 1944. He continued to refine his design—which superficially resembled Louis Breguet's gyroplane of the 1930s—until 1946, when a crack-up in his latest model convinced him that he was on the wrong track. Adopting the proven tail-rotor approach, he devised a twin-bladed main rotor similar to the ones used on the Bell helicopter. By 1948 his small and agile Model 360 had been certified by the CAA, and Hiller was on his way to becoming a youthful manufacturing mogul with big orders from military as well as civilian customers.

Still greater strides were taken in the late 1940s when Charles Kaman adapted the intermeshing rotor principle used by Anton Flettner on his *Kolibri*. The resulting craft was exceptionally easy to fly and could be held in a hover without problem. As head aerodynamicist at the Hamilton-Standard Propellers Division of United Aircraft, Kaman had loyally offered the idea to his employer, but was turned down—presumably because United had determined to stick with Sikorsky's single-rotor concept. Kaman then struck out on his own, setting up a factory in a former gymnasium near Hartford, Connecticut. Impressed by the performance of a Kaman prototype, the Navy, the Air Force and the Marines placed orders for production models.

Thus by the end of the 1940s, American armed forces had begun to adopt the helicopter. Aircraft that could land almost anywhere, hover motionless and fly close to the ground intrigued the military, despite the lavish care required to keep them flying, the shaking and shuddering, the slow speed and sometimes pitifully small payloads. Hundreds of helicopters were purchased for rescue operations, reconnaissance missions, the laying of communications wire across rugged

An idea that barely got off the ground

During World War II, both the U.S. Army and Navy encouraged the development of small, one-man helicopters with an eye toward deploying them as scouts or to ferry troops into otherwise inaccessible areas. Powered by tiny air-cooled engines and weighing just a few hundred pounds, these pint-sized flying machines were still in the experimental stage when that conflict ended, and they never saw combat. But after the War, a number of enterprising manufacturers laid plans to market civil versions of the craft, amid predictions of 70,000 sales a year and a minicopter in every American garage.

Several factors kept these rosy forecasts from becoming reality. For one, the minicopters turned out to be nearly as complicated and expensive to manufacture and maintain as full-sized machines. Moreover, they were quite impractical for the kind of weekend errand running touted in industry brochures. Their limited lifting ability would have been sorely taxed by the smallest bag of groceries, even if there had been a place to put it.

It took the skills of a Buck Rogers to fly the temperamental machines—one reason the Army eventually scrapped the idea—and experienced helicopter pilots warned that the craft would become "backyard death-traps in the hands of amateur aviators." The minicopter idea died with the onset of the postwar recession and would have probably foundered anyway simply because, as one pilot put it, "anyone smart enough to learn to fly one should have had sense enough not to."

The twin-rotor Hoppi-copter, which was built in the United States, was powered by a 35-hp engine and had a lightweight tubular framework.

A dapper aviator models the strap-on helicopter of French designer George Sablier. But it is not known whether the machine ever flew.

An amphibious minicopter prototype designed in the early 1950s for military use is put through its paces by its stand-up pilot.

terrain and for other tasks that were hazardous or impossible without them. But as quick as American military leaders were to embrace the helicopter, events would move quicker. Soon the armed services would find a pressing need for many hundreds more helicopters in a war that no one expected.

On the 25th of June, 1950, North Korean troops swarmed across the 38th Parallel, the dividing line between the Communist People's Republic of Korea to the north and the Republic of Korea to the south. Branded as aggressors by the United Nations Security Council, the invaders were opposed not only by the South Koreans but by the United States and by troops from 14 other outraged nations. By August, the allied forces commanded by American General Douglas A. MacArthur had checked the onslaught along a defensive perimeter around the South Korean port city of Pusan. Meanwhile, U.S. military pilots had begun to demonstrate what the helicopter could do in a combat situation.

In the years since World War II, military planners had given considerable thought to the role of the helicopter on the battlefield. But their projections were based primarily on a nuclear war, not the kind of conventional conflict that would be waged in the mountainous country of Korea. The Marines, using Frank Piasecki's Flying Bananas, had experimented with the radical notion of vertical envelopment—dropping troops into combat by helicopter. The Army, though interested in the new craft, was prevented by a ridiculous bit of bureaucracy from integrating it into battlefield operations. When the Army Air Forces were split off in 1947 to become the separate Air Force, the Army's remaining aviation sections were restricted to aircraft weighing two tons or less. The Banana weighed two and a half tons.

The few helicopters available at the outbreak of hostilities were mainly used by troop commanders to scout the unfamiliar and difficult terrain. But in early August, just six weeks after the fighting began, helicopters were pressed into action to fill another desperate need—the swift transport of badly wounded soldiers from the front lines to field hospitals. Most of the craft in service at this point were Sikorsky S-51s designed to accommodate a pilot and copilot, along with three passengers on a cramped bench to the rear. They were ill-suited for duty as aerial ambulances, but resourceful ground crews adapted them for lifesaving missions by removing a window and installing straps on the other side of the cabin to secure the handles of a stretcher. Carried in this makeshift fashion, a wounded soldier protruded out the window from about the knees down.

The first such medical evacuation took place on August 4, when a Marine helicopter flew out one casualty of a fire fight along the Pusan perimeter; five more were evacuated the next day, some of them plucked from hillsides too steep for a jeep to climb. On August 6 an Air Force pilot landed his copter at an aid station atop a 3,000-

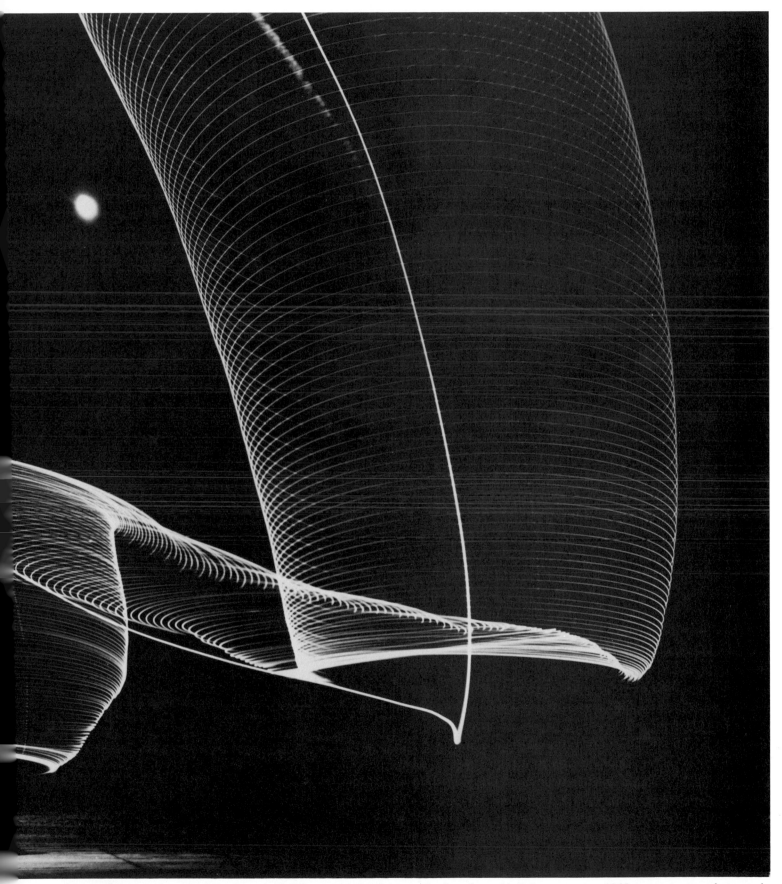

Lights on the tips of a night-flying Sikorsky S-51's rotor blades dramatically chart the craft's flight pattern in a 1949 time-exposure photograph.

foot hill surrounded by North Korean forces, picked up a seriously wounded soldier and whisked him to a hospital. The stage now was set for one of the most dramatic and important large-scale uses of the helicopter in the Korean War.

In the wake of World War II, the Army Medical Corps had revamped its plans for battlefield casualty care to take advantage of advances in medicine and surgical techniques. So that the wounded could be put speedily under a surgeon's care, Mobile Army Surgical Hospital—MASH—units were established. These were designed to place a team of surgeons and anesthesiologists, plus the necessary nurses, medical corpsmen and equipment, within earshot of enemy artillery. The first MASH unit to go into action went ashore at Pusan on July 6, just 11 days after the North Korean invasion. By the first days of August two more MASH units were serving in Korea. MASH surgeons often had to work around the clock; within the first six months, nearly 62,000 members of the United Nations forces would be wounded.

But the rugged Korean terrain and harsh weather proved an impediment. The overland transport of wounded troops was made agonizingly slow by the hills, flash floods, snowstorms and the primitive jeep-jolting roads. The poignant contrast between speedy medevac—short for medical evacuation—helicopter missions and land transport soon convinced Army medics on the scene that ambulance helicopters could enable the MASH teams to save many more lives.

The Army's first shipment of medevac helicopters to Korea—Bell 47s that had been fitted with a cocoon-like stretcher pod on each landing skid outrigger—were assigned directly to MASH units in mid-December, 1950. Their pilots did not have to wait long before going into action. On December 31, Chinese troops—who had entered the War on the North Korean side in November—launched a major offensive against United Nations positions. Two days later, Lieutenants Joseph L. Bowler and Willis G. Strawn picked up four severely wounded soldiers and brought them back to a MASH unit in their Bell 47s.

The bitter fighting continued, but the number of helicopters committed to MASH duty never numbered more than a dozen or so. Casualties were frequently so high that helicopters assigned to other duties were pressed into service. Chopper rides were reserved for only the more seriously injured—those with what came to be called a "helicopter wound." The MASH pilots did not have to be told that their work was vital: Before the Bell 47s arrived on the scene in numbers, 10 to 14 hours were needed to haul a wounded soldier to the nearest MASH station, and many died before reaching it. Now, troops felled by enemy bullets or shrapnel were arriving at MASH units within an hour of being hit.

The success of medevac helicopters prompted a wide-ranging realignment of U.S. military medical priorities. Before helicopters came into play, military surgeons had been trained to practice triage. This involved placing the wounded in one of three categories as soon as they arrived at an aid station: the walking wounded, men who could care for themselves and perhaps even return to the fight after minimum aid; men with serious but not immediately life-threatening wounds; and those needing massive and immediate medical care to preserve life. In traditional triage, the frontline medic and surgeon were trained to treat the walking wounded first, those who could be stabilized for the jarring jeep ride back to a base hospital second and the seriously wounded last. Triage was founded on the brutally realistic view that the frontline surgeon could save three or four wounded in the second category in the time required to treat one in the third.

The helicopter changed all this. If life could be preserved and a helicopter found, even the most gravely wounded could quickly be placed in the hands of a fully equipped surgical team. Henceforth, those in the third category were to receive first priority, with the result that battlefield mortality dropped dramatically.

The atmosphere of a MASH unit was generally frantic as helicopters brought in the wounded and surgical teams worked feverishly to save them. A roaring fire pit that blazed 24 hours a day added a macabre touch. Trash kept the flames alive. If a mobile hospital had to pack up and move in a hurry because of shifting battle lines, stockpiles of winter clothes might be tossed into the blaze, to deny them to the enemy. As in earlier wars, though not as often, the price a soldier paid for life could be an arm or a leg. MASH pilot Joseph Bowler recalled after a violent enemy offensive that in his unit's fire pit "they were burning mostly arms and legs from amputations from wounds and frozen limbs."

Bowler and his fellow pilots frequently volunteered to fly medevac missions for which their choppers were not equipped. Night flights were especially tricky. The Bell 47s lacked instrument panel lights, and pilots—with both hands on the controls—had to read the dials

A wounded soldier lies strapped beneath the lid of a litter pod attached to the fuselage of a Sikorsky S-51. The S-51, which became the workhorse of Marine and Air Force rescue operations during the first year of the Korean War, could carry a pilot, a medic and two patients.

and gauges by the glow of a flashlight gripped between their knees. In rain or darkness, with no windshield wipers and only rudimentary landing lights, they flew with their heads thrust out the side. They also had to cope with their wounded passengers. They rigged up heaters for the stretcher pods and installed transfusion systems to administer plasma or whole blood to keep the men from bleeding to death or dying of shock in flight. The transfusion bottles hung inside the cabin, and pilots cut holes in the helicopter sidewalls to thread the tubes through to the outside pods. When the cold Korean air blasting through these make-shift openings proved too uncomfortable, one resourceful captain flattened some beer cans and used them to fashion little spring-loaded doors to cover the holes.

Helicopter pilots in Korea were generally forbidden to fly where they were likely to come under enemy fire. Their machines were in short supply, had no armor and carried no weapons to defend themselves with. Nonetheless, many helicopters were fired on and hit, and some

Marines at a forward battle area in Korea rush a wounded comrade toward a waiting Bell 47 helicopter. The aluminum platform litter mounted on the chopper's landing skid will be fitted with a plexiglass windscreen (on the ground by the skid) to protect the patient's head and shoulders in transit.

crashed, though not always as a consequence of bullet holes. One of the first choppers to be lost in Korea went down in the autumn of 1950 when the pressure from its rotor wash set off a powerful enemy antitank mine from 300 feet up. There were times, though, when a mission was so important that a helicopter would be dispatched into harm's way no matter the risk.

In the middle of March, 1951, Air Force Captain Joseph D. Cooper was putting a new helicopter through its final flight tests at Florida's Eglin Air Force Base. Destined for service in Korea, the craft was a Sikorsky model S-55, designated the H-19 by the Air Force; its two-man cockpit was mounted atop a cabin designed to accommodate 10 combat-equipped soldiers or a medical corpsman and eight stretcherborne casualties. Suddenly, special orders arrived from Korea; Cooper and the H-19 were hastily put aboard a huge C-124 Globemaster transport plane and rushed to Japan. There, Joe Cooper climbed into the H-19's cockpit and flew the hefty helicopter across the Sea of Japan to an air base in South Korea.

At the base, the hastily summoned pilot was personally briefed by the commander of the Fifth Air Force, General Earl E. Partridge, who informed Cooper that reconnaissance planes had spotted a Russian-built MiG-15 jet fighter that had crash-landed in North Korean territory with relatively little damage. It lay about 35 miles inland from the western coast of Korea, at the bottom of a box canyon 300 feet deep. American aerial combat experts were eager to obtain a MiG-15 and analyze its secrets. First put into combat the previous November, the new craft was swift and highly maneuverable—though U.S. pilots, with their superior training and an excellent fighter of their own in the F-86 Sabrejet, had shot several down with relative ease in dogfights over North Korea. Cooper's mission: to fly his H-19 to the downed plane and bring the key parts of the enemy craft back for examination.

The H-19 was designed to lift a maximum load of 2,000 pounds, and the best American estimate was that the crippled MiG-15 was more than four times that heavy. Even so, Cooper was ordered to proceed. Partridge made it clear that a chance to inspect even a few crucial parts of this formidable jet warplane would be well worth any damage done to the H-19.

On the bitterly cold afternoon of March 19, Cooper and his copilot lifted off from the base and headed for their jumping-off point, a small island in the Yellow Sea. Below them in the chopper's cabin were a demolition team of six thin, small South Korean soldiers, deliberately chosen for their slightness; an American jet fighter expert; and special tools for dismantling the MiG. Cooper stayed for just 30 minutes at the island, taking on fuel and rechecking the H-19 for expendable weight. To lighten the craft, he removed the parachutes and, in a last-minute decision, ordered one of the South Korean soldiers to remain behind. Even so, with its tanks full—and with extra fuel stowed on board in special nylon bags—the H-19 was 500 pounds overweight when it left the island.

Cooper flew low above the water until reaching shore, then climbed to 5,000 feet for the inland leg. The MiG was easy to spot, sitting in the open with its nose bashed in; an umbrella of 50 Air Force fighters guided the H-19 in and then wheeled overhead for protection. As Cooper landed, his passengers leaped out and ran with their tools to remove the engine and tail section, the two components of greatest interest to analysts in the United States.

As Cooper waited on the ground, engine running, he heard explosions and was certain that a North Korean onslaught had begun. Then the copilot ran to the helicopter and told him what was happening—the resourceful expert was attacking the MiG with saws and special explosives he had brought along to speed the work if it bogged down. The demolition crew loaded parts of the tail and the engine, which by this time had been reduced to a size that the Koreans could lift, into the helicopter, and Cooper prepared to take off—without the demolition team. The plan called for them to hike the several miles to friendly territory.

Though the helicopter had burned off a considerable amount of fuel—loading the pieces of the MiG had taken 35 minutes longer than expected—Cooper figured that the H-19 was still about half a ton heavier than it should be. Just getting off the ground would be a test of the chopper's capabilities.

Cooper managed to coax the overladen H-19 into the air and lumber forward at a low level—directly toward a 300-foot wall of the canyon. There was no chance of flying over it, so Cooper wheeled the struggling craft around and took off in the opposite direction, barely clearing a lower-lying stand of trees. The immediate danger past, Cooper started to climb. It took more than 10 minutes for the H-19 to reach 5,500 feet, and by then Cooper and his team realized that they had been seen, as ragged bursts of antiaircraft fire exploded close by, filling the sky with puffs of smoke and jarring the craft violently.

Dodging the flak as best he could in his heavily laden copter, Cooper shoved the throttle forward, pushed the nose into a shallow dive and sped out of danger, with the machine shaking vigorously. Cooper feared more than once that they were as good as dead. Somehow the helicopter held together, and Cooper landed his crew safe and sound on the island in the Yellow Sea. There the MiG parts were transferred to a Grumman SA-16 amphibian for the first leg of an express trip to the United States for study. Meanwhile, Cooper found that the main rotor of the H-19 had brought back its own souvenir of the mission—a hunk of shrapnel protruding from one of the three blades.

On March 23, four days after Cooper's return, General Matthew B. Ridgway sent 3,300 airborne troops to Monsan-Ni, near the 38th Parallel, in hopes of blocking the retreat of 15,000 Chinese. Cooper in his H-19—now fitted with new blades and gearbox—joined a steady stream of smaller H-5s in lifting out 148 soldiers who had been hurt in the parachute drop or wounded in the fighting, which, it turned out, was light, since the retreating Chinese had slipped away. The lone H-19 could evacuate the wounded at four times the rate of the older, smaller helicopters, taking 16 casualties from the drop zone in two quick trips while bringing in a three-quarter-ton load of medical supplies. In the following weeks—with time out for an engine overhaul—the H-19 chalked up a total of 93 evacuations of wounded and also rescued six downed fighter pilots.

The utility of bigger, wider-ranging choppers in the Korean War was ever more obvious. But the build-up was painfully slow. As the fighting continued, badly wounded men by the thousands were carried out by Army, Navy, Air Force and Marine pilots in the smaller Sikorskys, Hillers and Bells; finally, the Marines acquired a small fleet of what they called HRSs—their version of the Air Force's Sikorsky H-19. By September the Marines were using the new copters for medevac pickups and utility missions; then they began dropping tons of supplies and landing troops on the peaks of some of Korea's wildest mountains and razorback ridges at the front.

A Marine sprints back to a waiting Sikorsky S-55 after launching a rocket at the enemy in Korea. Since fixed rocket-launching sites were vulnerable, helicopters carried Marines with portable launchers to within range of their targets; the troops disembarked, fired the weapons, then took off again before the enemy could respond.

On October 11 the Leathernecks wrote a new chapter in military history with Operation *Bumblebee,* the first battalion-strength helicopter lift of troops. Nearly 1,000 Marines, relief for a weary unit that had taken its turn in the trenches, were loaded in successive waves into a dozen HRSs; over a period of nearly six hours, the choppers made a total of 156 flights, leapfrogging the cruel, grueling terrain. Their destination was the top of a 3,000-foot mountain, 15 miles from the loading base. When the first helicopters arrived near the peak, they hovered there as entire chopperloads of Marines in full combat gear scurried down knotted ropes in just 20 seconds and began immediately to clear the landing areas, situated just behind U.N. lines. Later waves of the choppers could then touch down and disgorge their troops in just 15 seconds. The operation went like clockwork and would have profound implications for future airborne actions.

By the end of 1951, the big Marine helicopters were lifting 2,000 men and 75 tons of supplies a month, and the numbers and tonnages grew during 1952 and in 1953, when one Marine helicopter squadron would haul 800 tons of supplies in five days. In the meantime, the Army—ignoring the 1947 restriction on the weight of its aircraft—had ordered a fleet of troop-carrying Piasecki and Sikorsky helicopters and committed itself to the concept of "airmobility," much to the delight of the foot soldier, who would be spared wearying marches and bone-jarring rides by truck.

Far more exciting than transporting masses of troops, however, was the use of helicopters to pluck downed fliers out of danger, as Marine Major David Cleeland learned on a cold March day in 1953.

Piloting a propeller-driven Corsair fighter on a rocket attack against a North Korean bridge, Cleeland had been hit by ground fire and forced to make a wheels-up landing on a frozen lake 60 miles behind enemy lines. The plane touched down heavily on its belly and then spun wildly across the ice; when it finally came to a halt, Cleeland found himself caught between enemy troops on both sides of the lake. Overhead, a fellow Corsair pilot radioed for a helicopter rescue team as Cleeland scurried for refuge behind his Corsair's fuselage, where he concocted a makeshift dummy out of his parachute, put his flying helmet on it and diverted the fire of enemy marksmen.

Cleeland had been huddling next to his crippled plane for close to an hour when an Air Force H-19 came whirling in to pick him up. But just as the chopper appeared, an armed Chinese horseman began galloping across the ice toward the downed flier. Then another fighter, which had been circling above the lake to mark Cleeland's position, streaked down and blasted the soldier out of the saddle.

Now the H-19 set down gently on the ice just 15 feet away from Cleeland's plane. Cleeland was reluctant to dash through the gantlet of enemy rifle fire that whistled around his Corsair and the waiting H-19; from the chopper's open cargo door, Airman Thomas C. Thornton shouted encouragement over the clatter of the spinning rotor blades. Finally, Cleeland jumped to his feet and ran toward Thornton's outstretched hand. A bullet smashed into Cleeland's leg, but he kept moving. Then another bullet ripped through Thornton's extended hand. Scarcely hesitating, Thornton stuck out his other hand and pulled Cleeland aboard, and the pilot lifted them into the welcome safety of the sky.

Four months after this bold rescue mission, the interminable peace talks, which had begun two years earlier in July 1951, at last produced an uneasy truce, and the three-year Korean War finally came to a close. Throughout the struggle, helicopters had proved themselves useful beyond the wildest dreams of the military planners in Washington. In their medevac role alone, helicopters lifted approximately 30,000 casualties from the battlefield—with a resulting drop in the death rate among the wounded.

This performance had been achieved with craft that were still, even at best, in the Model T stage of technical development. Indeed, the helicopter was sometimes described as "1,000 parts flying in close formation." Keeping this formation in the air presented a formidable challenge to helicopter pilots. As one early veteran advised a neophyte, controlling a chopper was "a lot like milking a nervous cow. You just get the controls in your hands and hang on while the ship jumps up and down." If the pilot so much as took his hand off the stick, the H-19s and HRSs then in action could go out of control. To tame the unruly machines, the Navy and Sikorsky were working on an automatic pilot that would enable the pilot to relax in flight. Lamentably, it would not be perfected in time for use in Korea.

Soon, however, a whole new generation of larger and more docile helicopters—Kaman, Piasecki and Sikorsky models—would be ready for use. And American military planners, when determining how best to employ these craft in battle, could draw on the examples of other nations as well as on their own combat experiences in Korea.

In March 1954, less than a year after the Korean armistice, Communist-led Viet Minh guerrilla forces surrounded the key French military base of Dienbienphu, in northern Vietnam. There, France was making a desperate stand in its eight-year bid to retain control of Indochina, a French colony since the 19th Century.

Helicopters had first been introduced into the conflict in 1950, when a pair of American-made Hiller 360s—three-seaters with stretcher pods bolted to their fuselages—were put into service as aerial ambulances. Flown by bold pilots—including a valiant woman *(pages 114-115)*—these two Hillers set a durable example for future French helicopter operations in Indochina. The 42 choppers that saw duty in the War— among them several more Hillers and some Sikorsky H-5s and H-19s—were used almost exclusively for medical evacuation missions. And one of the few exceptions to this rule had a grim outcome.

During the first week of the siege of Dienbienphu, helicopters bearing Red Cross insignia flew in to remove a group of marooned French pilots. The watching insurgents could plainly see that the men were uninjured, and that the French were thus violating time-honored international agreements that barred the transport of nonwounded combatants in vehicles with Red Cross markings. Not long afterward, when the craft returned to evacuate actual casualties, Communist gunners opened fire. At first, their aim was poor, but four days later they scored a direct hit on a French helicopter that had just lifted off from the roof of one of the hospitals. Chunks of the shattered chopper rained on another helicopter close behind it, and this second craft went down to a crash landing and burst into flames. The pilot was pulled out alive, but his wounded passenger perished in the blazing wreckage. Soon afterward, the French determined that further helicopter flights to and from Dienbienphu were hopeless.

The end of helicopter evacuation of the wounded only heightened the sense of doom that had settled over the beleaguered French garrison. As the fighting wore on, soldiers who had survived the loss of just one eye or one arm were returned to the firing line. Hundreds and then thousands of men with worse wounds had to be cared for on the spot rather than be moved out by helicopter. Finally, after nearly two months of bombardment and massed hand-to-hand assaults, the insurgents had tightened their grip until, on May 7, 1954, the Frenchmen surrendered. Nearly 11,000 men, many of them wounded, were taken prisoner, and France's dominion in Indochina came to an end.

In the United States, meanwhile, the Army and the Marines were both studying how they could best employ the helicopter on future battlefields. The Marines—encouraged by the success of their own troop lifts in Korea—continued to draw up plans and conduct field tests aimed at exploiting the helicopter's potential. But these efforts were hampered by disagreements within the top command over how far choppers should go in replacing waterborne landing craft in the Marines' traditional mission of mounting amphibious assaults on enemy shores. The Army also pursued a zigzag course of dramatic field experiments, hesitant development and tactical dispute. To enthusiasts, the helicopter appeared to be the obvious replacement for all or most paratroop and gliderborne operations, but doubters held that helicopters by nature would always be frail machines that should be kept beyond the combat, safely out of the range of enemy fire.

Complicating these conceptual conflicts was the military's uncertainty about how greatly helicopter performance could be improved, and how soon. And copter makers themselves were groping to find the right course of hardware development, using as their compass the wavering guidance of military planners who, to complete the circle of confusion, did not yet know for certain the kinds of missions to which the machines might ultimately be assigned.

To be sure, helicopter builders were not solely dependent on military

A French angel of mercy

"I probably came to the Army through my spirit of adventure," Valérie André once told an interviewer. And who would deny it? When she joined the French Army in 1948, fresh out of medical school, she was already an experienced parachutist and had been flying airplanes since she was 16.

After serving a year with the French Expeditionary Force in Indochina, Dr. André trained as a helicopter pilot in France, then returned to the war zone, where she was placed in command of a medevac squadron based near Hanoi.

In her American-made Hiller, Dr. André flew solo ambulance missions to isolated jungle outposts spread from the Gulf of Tonkin to the Laotian border. She rescued 165 wounded all told—and in saving lives, continually risked her own. She was often shot at as she flew over enemy positions, and ambush was an ever-present danger as she touched down in thickly vegetated areas. Even her patients could pose a hazard. One soldier, delirious from a head wound, grabbed her while the helicopter was airborne, threatening to bring the flight to a disastrous end. While still maneuvering the craft, she gave him a shove that sent him flying into a corner.

After 120 such missions, Dr. André inevitably showed the strain. Suffering from combat fatigue, she was sent home to France in 1953. But six years later she was in the thick of it again, this time serving as a flying doctor in Algeria, bringing her total of combat missions to 485.

Algeria was Dr. André's last war, but it was not the end of her service in the Army. Her bravery and devotion, which had earned her various decorations (below, right), also brought her steady advancement: From captain she rose to the rank of general in April 1976.

French Army Captain Valérie André, a rated helicopter pilot as well as a physician, stands before the Hiller 360 she flew on medical missions during the war in Indochina.

General Jean de Lattre de Tassigny, commander of French forces in Indochina, awards Dr. André the Croix de Guerre in 1952. Among other heroic feats, she was cited for parachuting into an outpost in Laos to treat a gravely wounded soldier.

Aided by Senegalese stretcher bearers, who had been recruited in Africa by the French, Dr. André unloads a wounded soldier at Lanessan Hospital in Hanoi.

markets. As soon as production-line models became available in the late 1940s, civilian customers began employing them in a variety of ways. By the early 1950s, helicopters were commonly used in such diverse applications as crop-dusting, surveying for oil and minerals, inspecting pipelines and power lines, flying police patrols and even herding cattle. A number of helicopter airlines had sprung up, beginning with a pioneering passenger service launched by British European Airways in June 1950. But the copters of the day were slow, extremely noisy and incapable of hauling sufficient payloads to make them truly profitable as commercial air carriers. Their civilian utility was thus somewhat limited, and the military still seemed the best place for helicopters to prove their mettle.

Through the 1950s, though, the controversies over the helicopter's combat role droned on without decisive resolution. In June 1956, Colonel Jay Vanderpool, a high-spirited and resourceful staff officer at the Army Aviation School at Fort Rucker, Alabama, obtained quiet approval from helicopter-minded superiors to do something about tipping the balance of the dispute. With no funding or formal charter, and under orders to avoid publicity, Vanderpool and a handful of subordinates put together a patchwork fleet of miscellaneous helicopters. Onto these they strapped a jumbled assortment of machine guns and rockets. Vanderpool then pressed several more men into service and formed a "Sky-Cav Platoon" that proceeded to engage in spectacular, earsplitting field tests. The behavior of the weapons, which had been designed for different conditions, could not always be predicted, yet the makeshift tests showed that supposedly fragile choppers could be transformed into mobile platforms for delivering devastating firepower to shield troops of a helicopter assault force.

Vanderpool's flying platoon gradually earned official approval and was enlarged to company strength for expanded experiments and exhibitions. But this small triumph did not decide the overall dispute. Choppers were still being accepted far too slowly to satisfy their adherents, while critics persisted in ridiculing the Sky-Cav innovators as "Vanderpool's Fools." Soon, however, the issue would be settled beyond doubt in combat, in a distant conflict that would become known as the "Helicopter War." ～

Royal Marine commandos practice helicopter assault tactics during Operation Sandfly, a 1962 British military exercise held in the Libyan desert.

A new, powerful breed

In the era of piston engines, helicopters flew with laborious slowness, shaken by a St. Vitus's dance of vibration. And even large ones carried disappointingly small payloads. But in the 1950s, an advance in helicopter design occurred that sparked a revolution. Though Americans created the first of the new helicopters, the Kaman K-225 synchropter, the French built the first one sold in any quantity: Sud Aviation S.E. 3130 Alouette II *(right).*

The difference between the new machines and their piston-engined forerunners was the source of power, a jet engine called a turboshaft. The engine installed in the Alouette, a 400-hp Turboméca Artouste II, was primitive by today's standards. Yet it was less than half the weight of a piston engine of the same output and small enough to mount on top of the helicopter, making for a roomier cabin. Moreover, it was self-cooling, ran with silky smoothness on inexpensive kerosene instead of costly aviation fuel and it could be operated at full power while the Alouette hovered, a practice that would ruin a piston engine.

The turboshaft was the engine helicopter designers had been waiting for. Refined and enlarged, it became the essential ingredient that made possible the host of helicopters shown on these and the following pages.

SUD AVIATION S.E. 3130 ALOUETTE II (1955)
The Alouette II could carry four passengers besides the pilot and fly at better than 100 mph. The aircraft's turboshaft engine, which run at a speed of 35,000 rpm, was slowed by a train of reduction gears so that the rotor would turn at a mere 350 rpm.

BELL UH-1N (1969)
This twin-engined version of the famous Huey, flown by the U.S. Marines in Vietnam, is armed with two six-barrel, Gatling-style miniguns, able to fire 4,000 rounds per minute. The wires that zigzag along the boom are long-range radio antennas.

WESTLAND WASP (1962)
Built to attack submarines, Britain's all-weather Wasp had main-rotor blades that folded parallel to the boom for stowage aboard ship. Casters on the undercarriage made the single-engined helicopter easy to maneuver on deck.

BOEING VERTOL CH-47C CHINOOK (1967)
The twin-engined Chinook—here in U.S.
Army colors—could carry 20,000
pounds suspended from the cargo hook
under the fuselage. It could set down as
easily on water as land; buoyant pods along
the craft's sides helped to keep it afloat.

SIKORSKY HH-53C JOLLY GREEN GIANT (1967)
The Jolly Green Giant, which rescued
hundreds of downed fliers during the
Vietnam War, could fly 200 mph or faster in
an emergency. The range of this twin-
engined craft could be extended virtually
without limit by in-flight refueling
through the extendable probe in its nose.
It also had external fuel tanks that could
be jettisoned to lighten the load.

MIL MI-12 (1969)
The Soviet Mi-12 is the largest helicopter in the world. Powered by four 6,500-hp turboshaft engines, it can lift a payload of 55,000 pounds—nearly twice the capacity of the Sikorsky HH-53C.

CCCP 21142

AGUSTA 109A (1971)
Designed and built in Italy, the streamlined Agusta 109A is unusual among light-duty helicopters for its retractable landing gear. By helping to reduce drag, this feature contributes to the craft's superior fuel economy despite two 400-hp engines.

BELL JETRANGER (1966)
This jet-age successor to Bell's 47-series utility helicopter (page 96) is just as versatile but can fly 40 mph faster, has a greater range and can carry a bigger payload. In the 15 years following its introduction, approximately 4,000 were sold for commercial use.

MIL MI-24 D (1975)

Designed originally to transport eight soldiers into combat, the Soviet Mi-24 was redesigned as a gunship, with the gunner sitting in the front cockpit, ahead of the pilot. Its armament includes 57-mm. rockets and a four-barrel 12.7-mm. machine gun under the nose.

HUGHES AH-64 (1975)

Conceived specifically as a tank killer, this U.S. Army attack helicopter boasts rockets and laser-guided missiles with ranges greater than three miles. There is also a 30-mm. cannon aboard that the pilot can aim simply by turning his head toward a target and framing it in a look-and-shoot gun sight attached to his helmet. The tips of the helicopter's rotor, which turns at 280 rpm, are bent to reduce high-speed buffeting.

A workhorse named Huey

The helicopter's military potential first became apparent in the Korean War, but it was not until the Vietnam War, a decade later, that it was fully realized. Of all the rotorcraft that served in Southeast Asia during that long, frustrating conflict, none was a more common or more welcome sight to troops fighting in flooded paddies and look-alike villages than the Bell UH-1, known universally as the Huey.

From 1962 onward, thousands of these ungainly craft took to the air daily in every type of weather to perform countless tasks, a number of which can be seen here and on the following pages. Some Hueys were especially fitted out for carrying assault troops into battle. Others, heavily armed with machine guns and rockets, protected the troops with withering fire into enemy positions. Hueys often provided the sole link between isolated outposts and the outside world, ferrying everything from mail to cases of cold beer to the men. Squadrons of medevac Hueys routinely flew into the thick of the fighting to pick up badly wounded soldiers and rush them to hospitals, thereby saving thousands of lives; and Hueys had the sad task as well of bringing back the bodies of men killed in action.

"The Huey was the workhorse of the Vietnam War," Donald Usher, a chopper pilot in that conflict, recalled. "More than any other aircraft, it came to symbolize the helicopter for our people and for the enemy alike."

Coming into a landing zone under intense enemy fire, an Army Huey dumps ammunition boxes to beleaguered South Vietnamese and prepares to evacuate the survivors. Bags on the ground contain the bodies of soldiers killed in action.

127

Starting out on a patrol in 1969, troops of the 101st Airborne Division jump from a Huey into a clearing too small for the chopper to land in.

A Huey medevac helicopter arrives with aid for 173rd Airborne Brigade troops who had been caught in an ambush near Saigon in October 1965.

A crew chief in the doorway of a 1st Cavalry Division Huey troopship lays down a barrage with his M-60 machine gun.

Troops of the 1st Cavalry Division stand on the skids of their Huey transports, ready to jump off when the helicopters slow to a hover. The billow of white smoke is the residue of a phosphorous shell fired to signal the end of an artillery bombardment intended to soften up enemy positions.

5

Helicopter War

Two days before Christmas, 1961, the tropical tranquillity of the Vietnamese countryside west of Saigon was shattered by a strange, fearsome sound. Fluttering noisily over the shimmering paddies and the lacework of ancient canals were 30 lumbering U.S. Army Shawnee helicopters arrayed in a long, ragged line. They were setting out on what was in reality—official disclaimers and rules of engagement notwithstanding—a combat assault operation.

Such operations, of course, already had a history; the U.S. Marines had mounted "vertical assault" demonstrations even before the Korean War, and in 1956 the British at Suez had landed troops from helicopters on enemy positions. But this was the first time American helicopters had been used in a combat assault and the first time such an operation had been mounted in Vietnam—soon to become the scene of the helicopter's full coming of age as a weapon of war.

The tandem-rotor Shawnees flown in the operation were descendants of Frank Piasecki's original Flying Banana. In their plexiglass-enclosed noses sat U.S. Army pilots of the 57th Transportation Company (Light Helicopter), which had arrived in Vietnam only 11 days before. A U.S. Army crew chief stood in each helicopter's open cargo door, and inside, on canvas troop seats, were a dozen paratroopers of the Army of the Republic of Vietnam (ARVN), veterans of the already long and frustrating struggle with the Viet Cong guerrillas.

The mission's objective was a small village strung out along a tree-lined canal about a dozen miles west of Saigon. The village was thought to be the headquarters of a Viet Cong rifle company guarding a clandestine radio transmitter. Although the guerrillas were reportedly armed with small automatic weapons and a .50-caliber machine gun, the helicopters were unarmed except for submachine guns in the hands of the crew chiefs, who were under strict orders not to fire unless fired upon. The official hope was that the Viet Cong would refrain from shooting at the Shawnees to avoid drawing the Americans further into the War.

Minutes after lift-off, the choppers reached the prearranged landing zones—pineapple fields on either side of the canal. The formation split in two as the helicopters made for their assigned landing spots, then each one flared sharply, nose pointed skyward to kill off air speed, and hovered with its tires just above the soggy ground. The ARVN troops leaped from the helicopters and ran for the canal, firing as they went. The tree line along the canal began to sparkle with the muzzle flashes of

Silhouetted in the doorway of a Bell H-34 helicopter, an American machine gunner in Vietnam scans the rice paddies below for signs of enemy activity during a reconnaissance flight near Saigon in 1964.

return fire, and it was soon evident that the Viet Cong felt no compunction about shooting at the American aircraft.

As the last ARVN troopers jumped, the crew chiefs called "Clear," the pilots "pulled pitch" and all the helicopters banked away, noses down and accelerating hard. All, that is, except one—a chopper carrying a lieutenant colonel, who had come along as an observer.

The trouble started when the colonel, who had flown single-rotor helicopters but never a tandem-rotor craft, insisted on sharing the Shawnee's dual controls with the ship's commander, Chief Warrant Officer Robert Sword. Soon the colonel's interference was causing the helicopter to lurch erratically out of position. At the landing zone, the wayward craft overshot its approach, then overcorrected and planted one of its rear wheels firmly in the ooze of the sodden pineapple field. As Sword struggled to control the chopper, it pivoted around the mired wheel, lurching like a wild fowl caught in a snare. The craft finally toppled onto its side, fatally crushing an ARVN soldier and gravely injuring another in a spray of shattered wooden rotor blades.

The Americans scrambled clear of the crippled helicopter as the ARVN troops managed to suppress the Viet Cong fire. Minutes later, another Shawnee eased down to a low hover and picked up Sword, the colonel, the crew chief and the injured Vietnamese.

The 57th never learned the final result of its operation—whether any enemy leaders or radio transmitters had been captured. But despite the equivocal outcome and the loss of one Shawnee, the operation could still be declared a success. From the rapid deployment of the ARVN forces to the prompt rescue of the stranded crewmen and the injured Vietnamese, the men of the 57th had conclusively demonstrated the usefulness of the helicopter on the battlefield.

The size and importance of the role that the helicopter would ultimately assume in Vietnam would come as a surprise to all but a handful of visionaries. Even the pioneering helicopter enthusiasts in the Marine Corps and the Army could not have envisioned the range of tasks that helicopters would perform routinely at the height of the Vietnam War.

By the late 1960s, long-range Air Force helicopters, refueled in mid-air, would regularly rescue downed airmen under fire 500 miles and more from their bases. Huge flying cranes would carry damaged aircraft out of the jungle and back to base for repair. Helicopter troop transports would in some roles replace armored personnel carriers as infantry assault vehicles, just as helicopter gunships would break the fighter plane's monopoly on the close air support of embattled troops. And medevac helicopters would whisk wounded from the battlefield with merciful efficiency. In these and other roles, helicopters would become utterly indispensable to the conduct of modern warfare.

At the time of the 57th Transportation Company's initial helicopter assault in 1961, the full development of the helicopter's military potential was still several years off. Yet U.S. military planners already knew

Crewmen of a twin-rotored Shawnee assault helicopter downed by the Viet Cong keep a sharp lookout for guerrillas as a huge Sikorsky H-37 attempts to hoist the craft from a flooded paddy. Although capable of lifting 10,000 pounds, the H-37 failed in its salvage effort—the stricken helicopter was mired too deeply in the mud.

from the French experience in Vietnam that helicopters could be very useful in fighting the guerrilla-style war in which Americans were becoming increasingly involved.

In the previous decade, the Viet Cong's predecessors, the Viet Minh, had evolved a tactic that they used repeatedly to bleed the French white. They would attack an isolated French post in strength; the defenders would beat off the assault and call for help. The French would mount a relief column, which would proceed by road straight into the jaws of an ambush. After fighting its way out, the column would arrive at the besieged position only to find that the enemy had vanished.

Helicopters in numbers, their advocates argued, would drastically alter the terms of this tactical equation. Rather than taking days to arrive, fatigued and reduced in number, a relief force could be summoned up in hours or minutes. Instead of crawling along a predictable route, vulnerable to ambush and land mines, it could arrive from any direction at 100 miles per hour, fresh, at full strength and ready for battle.

The reasoning of the helicopter advocates proved sound. The U.S. and South Vietnamese forces did in fact come to rely on the helicopter for much of their mobility. And a brutal testing ground Vietnam was—for the machines, for their crews and for the tacticians who planned their deployment. Vietnam was basically a war without fronts; the Viet Cong could usually choose where and when to fight. The lush, tropical environment offered cover to the locally based insurgents and hazards to the helicopterborne Americans. In dense jungle, pilots might have to ease down through narrow-necked holes in the towering canopy of foliage into bottle-shaped openings that had been blasted out by explosives. Under the canopy, they had to find a landing spot or a place to hover low among the fallen trees and jagged stumps, where the helicopters were sitting ducks as they dropped off their troops or supplies.

On or near the ground, the soil itself could be a hazard. In many areas, it was a red clay called laterite that became bottomless glue when wet and crumbly rock when dry. Traffic of men and machines turned it to fine powder that could clog engines and sandblast rotor blades as it was churned up during takeoffs and landings. And everywhere over Southeast Asia, the very air, consistently hot and humid, sapped the strength of helicopter engines and the lifting power of rotors.

The North Vietnamese and the Viet Cong, moreover, became experts at wing-shooting choppers as they lumbered to and fro across the countryside. Enemy commanders issued specific instructions for downing the various types of craft. "The type used to carry troops," noted a document captured in 1963, "is very large and looks like a worm. It has two rotors and usually flies at an altitude of 200 to 300 meters. To hit its head, lead it by either one length or two thirds of a length when it flies horizontally. The type used to transport commanders or casualties looks like a ladle. Lead this type one length when in flight. It is good to fire at the engine section when it is hovering or landing."

Though all airmen in Vietnam faced danger almost as soon as they left the ground, the hazards braved by those who flew in helicopters seemed more immediate. Unlike their fighter- and bomber-flying colleagues, who usually entered battle at thousands of feet of altitude in sealed, air-conditioned cabins, helicopter crews flew relatively close to the ground and lived with the smell of sweat, kerosene, exhaust gases and gunpowder, the acrid stench of high explosives and, at times, the smell of blood. Few of them carried parachutes, since during the critical phase of a mission they would be too low to bail out anyway. The helicopter men could usually hear the guns that were shooting at them—and they could feel the impact of the rounds when they hit.

The early helicopters gave their crews precious little protection. The only armor a Shawnee carried was jury-rigged steel plating beneath the crew seats, installed as much for morale as for its bullet-stopping capability. And it did not take much to incapacitate some of the helicopters themselves. During the initial years of American involvement, the Viet Cong would plant spears in likely landing spaces, along with arrows set in bows that would be released automatically by the downdraft of a hovering chopper. These devices were intended chiefly for the disembarking troops rather than the helicopters, but they could damage the machines. The Shawnee's control cables and fluid lines were so open to battle damage that a story circulated among the men who flew the odd-looking craft that one had been downed by a hand-thrown spear.

Not all the helicopters that saw early action in Vietnam were so vulnerable as the Shawnee. The robust Sikorsky S-58, descended from the S-55 of the Korean War, was generally considered to be the most capable and dependable piston-engined helicopter ever built. Designed as a submarine hunter for the Navy but used in Vietnam principally by the Marines as an assault craft, the S-58 earned itself a permanent place in Corps slang through the corruption of the letters of its original Marine designation, HUS (for Helicopter, Utility, Sikorsky). HUS became the word "Huss," denoting not only the helicopter itself, but anything good or beneficial. To thousands of Marines who have never flown in an S-58 or even seen one, "Gimme a huss" is synonymous with "Do me a favor." So durable was the helicopter itself that the last model remained in service until 1969, long after a new generation of aircraft had taken over the main work of the Helicopter War.

The need for more advanced choppers was apparent almost from the start. Not only were craft like the Shawnee highly vulnerable to small-arms fire, but all the helicopters used at the beginning of the War, even the rugged Huss, were short on power. Their bulky piston engines had been enlarged and refined to the limits of technology, but they still could not produce the necessary lift. With Vietnam's steamy atmosphere further restricting their lifting power, even modest efforts to equip the craft with adequate armor or weaponry were doomed to failure.

A solution to the problem was at hand, however, in the turboshaft engine. This was a jet engine that used the powerful blast of expanding gases to spin a turbine that cranked a powershaft. The shaft, through a complex series of gears, turned the rotor in much the same way that jet engines spun the propellers on turboprop airliners such as the Vickers Viscount and Lockheed Electra. Turbines produced vastly more power for each pound of their own weight than did conventional piston engines and were far less bulky—small enough to fit under the main rotor hub rather than occupy half the fuselage. Their fuel consumption was high, but it was more than offset by the extra load capacity.

The first turbine helicopter was the Kaman K-225 synchropter, built in the United States by Charles Kaman from his earlier adaptation of Anton Flettner's World War II *Kolibri (page 93),* with a similar pair of intermeshing rotors. It appeared in 1951, but America's first production turbine helicopter was not available until 1958, when the Air Force bought a high-powered version of the K-225 for use as a pilot-rescue vehicle. The craft's unusual rotor system and odd shape made it the object of some amiable derision among the men who flew it. Its intermeshing rotors, they said, "looked like two palm trees trying to beat each other to death," and the wide, boxy fuselage needed to accommodate the twin rotors created noisy drafts, which led crews to ignore the helicopter's official name, Huskie, in favor of the more descriptive Whistling Outhouse. For all its ungainliness, however, the Huskie proved very stable in a hover, admirably suiting it to rescue work in Vietnam.

By the mid-1960s, a wide variety of turbine helicopters were serving in the expanding conflict. Boeing Vertol, successor to the company founded by Frank Piasecki in 1945, replaced the Shawnee with two powerful transports, both with Piasecki's characteristic tandem rotors. For the Navy and Marines, the firm built the CH-46 Sea Knight, which could operate from aircraft carriers—its rotor blades folded to facilitate parking in cramped spaces—and could carry 25 troops or a 6,600-pound load. For the Army, Vertol turned out the much larger CH-47 Chinook with a 45-troop capacity. One of these would sweep 147 refugees to safety in a single lift in the last tragic days of the War.

The champion heavyweight lifter, however, was Sikorsky's CH-54 Skycrane, whose twin turboshaft engines and huge six-bladed rotor enabled it to hoist and carry at 100 miles per hour objects as heavy as 25,000 pounds: a small tank, a 155-millimeter artillery piece, a bridge section or a downed aircraft. Of the 5,600 Army helicopters shot down in Vietnam, nearly two thirds were successfully retrieved, many by Skycranes. The CH-54's 90-foot fuselage had a bulbous cockpit, a tail rotor and little more than a skeletal boom in between, giving the craft the appearance of an enormous dragonfly. Loads were either suspended by cable from a hoist or enclosed in a container that the helicopter straddled with its widespread landing gear. One such container, called a people pod, was designed to function as a mobile command center or medical unit, or to carry 45 combat-equipped soldiers, though the Skycrane was capable of lifting one packed with nearly twice that number.

The smallest choppers in Vietnam were the Loaches (for Light Observation and Command Helicopter). Though the idea of such a reconnaissance craft was as old as the helicopter itself, the first Loach specially built for the purpose did not appear until 1966, when Hughes Helicopters won an Army design competition with its OH-6 Cayuse. An agile, compact craft used primarily to scout enemy positions, the OH-6 sometimes took full advantage of its maneuverability in a seemingly suicidal tactic known as "trolling for fire." Paired with a heavily armed helicopter gunship that flew some distance away, it would pass low over a suspected enemy stronghold, diving and darting to present a difficult but inviting target. Once shot at, the pilot would mark the spot the fire had come from with a colored smoke grenade and then back off as his gunship partner blasted away at the spot with rockets and cannon.

The Sikorsky company's principal turbine helicopters—heirs to the redoubtable Huss—were two large, twin-engined craft, the H-3 and H-53, which performed similar duties and became two of the most distinguished aircraft of the Helicopter War. Like the Huss, the H-3 was designed as a submarine hunter for the Navy; the larger, more powerful H-53 was developed a few years later for the Marines as an assault transport. While the H-3 could carry more than 20 troops, the H-53 had

A harrowing ride aboard Yankee Papa 13

Huddled on the flight line at Danang, Marine helicopter crews are briefed before the mission.

Life photographer Larry Burrows, who would die in Vietnam, had been on scores of helicopter missions, but none so harrowing as the one flown by Marine Helicopter Squadron 163 in April 1965.

The 163rd was to airlift a battalion of South Vietnamese troops to an area about 20 miles from Danang where intelligence reports indicated that enemy insurgents infiltrating from the north had set up a rendezvous point. Burrows flew to the site in a Sikorsky S-58, with the radio call sign "Yankee Papa 13," focusing his camera throughout the mission on Lance Corporal James C. Farley, the helicopter's 21-year-old crew chief.

"The Viet Cong were just waiting for us to come into the landing zone," Burrows later reported. "We were all like sitting ducks."

After depositing its soldiers on the ground, Yankee Papa 13 was sent back to Danang for more. On its next approach, the pilot, Captain Peter Vogel, spotted another chopper, "Yankee Papa 3," on the ground. With its engine still on and rotors turning, the ship was obviously in trouble. Vogel landed nearby and ordered Farley to aid the stricken craft's pilot. Burrows chased after him.

"A Viet Cong machine gun was spraying the area," Burrows said. "Farley scrambled up to the pilot and fought to drag him out but he couldn't be budged. Farley hastily examined the pilot. Through the blood around his face and throat, Farley could see a bullet hole in the neck. That, plus the fact that the man had not moved at all, led him to believe the pilot was dead."

Farley and Burrows raced back to their own chopper to find that the plexiglass had been shot out of the cockpit, a bullet had grazed the pilot's neck, and the radio and instruments were out of action. "We climbed fast and climbed fast the hell out of there," Burrows recalled. Safe at last in Danang, the photographer was accorded a rare honor for his part in the mission: a set of helicopter crewman's wings. "You've earned it," said the squadron's skipper.

Approaching the landing zone, crew chief James C. Farley opens fire with his M-60 machine gun at Viet Cong positions.

As Yankee Papa 13 touches down, South Vietnamese soldiers scramble through the doorway and fan out to join their comrades from other choppers. They were under orders to attack the Viet Cong firing from the tree line in the background.

On Yankee Papa 13's second trip, a wounded gunner from the downed Yankee Papa 3 runs toward Farley. After YP3's mortally wounded copilot staggered over, Farley and Burrows dashed to the stricken chopper to rescue the pilot.

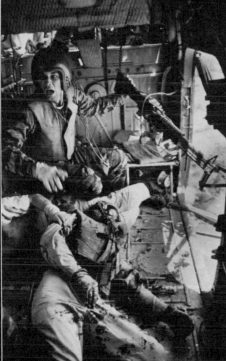

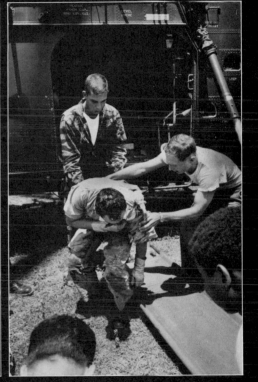

Disregarding the enemy's fire, Farley struggles to remove the pilot. After giving him up for dead, Farley and Burrows raced back to their own helicopter amid a hail of small-arms fire.

Just after lift-off, as YP3's copilot lies dying beside him, Farley shouts to a crewmate, "My gun is jammed! Cover your side—I'll help with these guys." YP3's wounded gunner lay slumped in the other doorway.

At the headquarters compound back at Danang, Yankee Papa 3's gunner is eased out of the helicopter by Farley and another Marine. The copilot, already dead of chest wounds, was carried away by other Marines.

On the way back to the squadron flight line,
Farley is overcome by grief over the death of YP3's
copilot and his inability to extricate the wounded
pilot. He later learned that the pilot was
still alive—rescued by another helicopter crew.

room for at least 30 and could lift almost as much as the Skycrane.

The size and power of the two Sikorsky craft made them natural choices for a new task that arose when American fighters and bombers began massive attacks on targets in North Vietnam early in 1965. American fliers downed by North Vietnamese antiaircraft guns, and later by surface-to-air missiles (SAMs), had to be retrieved from North Vietnam and neighboring Laos whenever possible. Long-range rescue operations were assigned to the U.S. Air Force Air Rescue Service in Saigon, and eventually came to involve teams of helicopters and planes from American bases in Thailand and northern South Vietnam and occasionally from carriers in the Gulf of Tonkin.

At the heart of each team was a pair of specially equipped Air Force H-3 or H-53 rescue helicopters, which, for their benign role, camouflage and imposing bulk were given the memorable nickname Jolly Green Giant. Both types of Jolly Green Giant were fitted with self-sealing fuel tanks and quarter-inch titanium armor plating to protect vital components, making the helicopters exceptionally battleworthy; on one occasion, an H-53 survived six hits by 20-millimeter armor-piercing ammunition. And by 1967, both the H-3 and H-53 had in-flight refueling probes that gave them virtually unlimited range.

In a typical rescue attempt, two Jolly Greens would fly to the area where the airman was thought to have gone down and there rendezvous with a pair of A-1s—large propeller-driven fighter-bombers nicknamed Dump Trucks by the Air Force for the three and a half tons of ordnance they could unload. Circling at a safe distance, well clear of enemy antiaircraft fire, would be a communications relay plane that supervised the operation by radio. In some cases, the communications plane was a specially adapted C-130 transport-tanker that could refuel the helicopters after they completed their pickup.

The downed flier was usually pinpointed with the aid of a homing radio beacon beamed from a tiny transmitter in his survival vest. When the aerial team reached him, they would instruct him by radio to "pop" a red smoke flare to reveal his exact location. Since the flare also revealed his position to the enemy, the rescue team would then have to work quickly. The A-1s would swoop low over the site and suppress any enemy ground fire by saturating the area with rockets, bombs, cannon fire and cluster bombs made up of antipersonnel bomblets ejected by the hundreds from canisters. The pair of helicopters would then move in for the rescue. One, the "low bird," made the pickup; the other, the "high bird," stood by in case something went wrong with the first—its presence ensuring immediate rescue for the low-bird crew, and thus encouraging them to attempt rescues that might otherwise have been unreasonably hazardous. Commonly, the low bird would winch down a 250-foot-long cable, on the end of which was a pointed cylinder called a jungle penetrator. It dropped like a plumb bob through the dense foliage to the downed airman, who pulled out an arm at its base, sat on it and held tight to the cylinder as he was hoisted to safety. If the airman was injured, a pararescueman would be lowered, perhaps with a rigid litter onto which he would strap the flier.

From the start of long-range rescue operations until the bombing of North Vietnam stopped early in 1973, the rescue teams maintained an extraordinary record of success. Of all downed American airmen who were able to contact a friendly aircraft on their survival radios after reaching the ground in North Vietnam or Laos, 80 per cent were recovered—and the 20 per cent lost included the many fliers who landed in densely populated areas and were captured almost immediately.

One reason the success rate was so high was that the teams were prepared to go to extraordinary lengths to effect a rescue. In one instance late in 1969, an Air Force F-4 went down over central Laos, and for two and a half days Rescue Control in Saigon dispatched a steady stream of Jolly Greens, A-1s, C-130s and jet fighters in 336 separate sorties from their bases hundreds of miles away in an attempt to recover the pilot and "back seater"—the plane's radar observer and weapons-systems operator. As it turned out, only the back seater was recovered, and in the process five A-1s were badly damaged, five Jolly Greens were so severely shot up that they had to be cannibalized for spare parts and a pararescueman was killed. The firepower employed during the rescue was equal to that used in many a small war. At one point jet fighters dropped white-phosphorous bombs in rows to create a smoke corridor that would screen rescue helicopters from enemy gunners; the quantity of munitions dumped was so great that the cloud they created was clearly visible in television transmissions from weather satellites.

The hazards of such rescue missions forged strong bonds between the fliers who took part in them; if one was shot down, the others would, as a matter of course, make every possible effort to save him. Knowing this, the pilot of a stricken rescue craft often tried to spare his friends the job of coming after him where he knew the risks to be too great. In the spring of 1966, at the end of an unsuccessful search for a downed airman, a low-flying rescue-team A-1 was hit in the wing by flak and set aflame. The pilot might have zoomed to sufficient altitude to bail out, but had he done so, he would have come down in an area infested with enemy guns—all of which, he knew, would have been trained on his friends when they came back for him. Instead, he chose to stay low to evade the guns, hoping to climb and bail out over a safe area. Before he reached safety, however, the flames burned through his aileron cables; the A-1 rolled and crashed from low altitude, and the pilot was killed, sacrificing himself to spare the helicopter crews under his protection.

The Jolly Green Giants' awesome capabilities and their long-range rescues made them famous, but the craft that ultimately came to symbolize the Helicopter War was less than one quarter the size of the larger of the Jolly Greens, and it performed all manner of duties, humble as well as heroic. When it first flew in 1956 at Bell Aircraft's Fort Worth plant, it was a simple, turbine-powered, single-rotor craft with room for four passengers and a cruising speed of 115 miles per hour. The Army bought it for general utility purposes, giving it the designation HU-1 (for Helicopter, Utility-1) and the official name Iroquois. The name never caught on among Army pilots, however. They came up with another, based on the helicopter's initials, and even after the Defense Department changed HU-1 to UH-1, the nickname stuck. The UH-1 was—and is—the Huey.

The craft soon proved exceptionally tough and reliable, and adaptable to a degree that neither Bell nor the Army could possibly have foreseen in the late 1950s. Over more than 20 years of full-scale production, Bell turned out a dozen different Huey models designed for a wide variety of tasks: One model set a rotorcraft speed record of 316 miles per hour in 1969, while another routinely carried 16 armed troops and flew at a gross weight of eight tons, nearly three times the maximum laden weight of the earliest models. At least 12,000 Hueys were produced, more than any other helicopter before or since, and more than any single type of fixed-wing military aircraft since World War II. A significant proportion of the total production was shipped to Vietnam; on any given day during the height of the War, more than 2,000 Hueys would be in the sky over Southeast Asia.

The first of these helicopters, Huey As, began to reach units in Vietnam in the spring of 1962. They were assigned to medevac duty, picking up where the Army's MASH helicopter units of the Korean War had left off. But the new aircraft and a very different form of combat changed the nature of the job. The Huey could carry three stretcher patients and a trained medic inside its cabin, rather than two wounded soldiers strapped to outside litters, as on the Bell 47, the Huey's Korean War predecessor. On the other hand, in this war without fronts, there were often no safe zones behind friendly lines where medevacs could take on their casualties, and there were no nearby mobile hospitals to carry them to. The Huey medevacs regularly had to fly straight into battle and dodge enemy fire to pick up their wounded, and then transport them all the way to base hospitals for treatment.

The medevac radio call sign, "Dustoff," became the common soldier's term for medevac units, and he always used it with respect. An early medevac team had selected Dustoff from an official list of call signs because the available alternatives all sounded too combative. Dustoff, some think, referred to the billowing cloud the medevacs' rotors stirred up. Regardless of its origin, however, Dustoff meant only one thing to the wounded soldier: salvation. He knew that whatever else might fail him in that endless, frustrating war, those olive drab Hueys painted with bright red crosses would not.

Not least of the risks in flying Dustoff missions was the red cross itself. The sanctity of this mercy symbol was violated by both sides. The enemy seldom respected it—as often as not they used the crosses as targets—and it was not unknown for cross-emblazoned Hueys to drop off ammunition before loading up with wounded ("preventive medicine'' one Dustoff pilot called it). But Dustoff helicopters almost never carried door guns, and the crews were fiercely committed to their medical responsibilities. Given a spot to land, Dustoff would try; the units would evacuate, under fire and without discrimination, Australians, South Koreans and Vietnamese—even wounded enemy soldiers who had been captured—as well as Americans.

Opportunities for selfless heroism were part of a Dustoff's daily routine. Major Charles L. ''Mad Man'' Kelly, for example, set the precedent for Dustoff's dedication to duty. A medevac commander early in the War, he would risk his life all day, then at night fly to isolated bases, lifting out any additional casualties that might have turned up in the meantime. Killed at the controls of his Huey while evacuating wounded in 1964, he was posthumously awarded the Distinguished Service Cross, the nation's second-highest decoration. The heliport at the Army medical center at Fort Sam Houston in Texas was named for him.

Another celebrated Dustoff pilot, Chief Warrant Officer Michael Novosel, was a World War II veteran and a commercial airline pilot with 16,000 hours of flight time before he reached Vietnam. During two tours of duty he evacuated 5,500 casualties. His son, Michael Jr., joined him on his second tour and picked up 2,500 himself, for a family total of 8,000. By contrast, the top medevac pilot in Korea had logged more than 1,000 saves—an indication not of his lesser achievement but of the vastly enlarged role and capability of helicopters in Vietnam.

Soon after the Huey began to arrive in Vietnam in 1962, a few were assigned to more combative duties than evacuating wounded. They were to defend troop-carrying helicopters during the critical landing phase of an assault. Planes—even the World War II-vintage propeller-driven bombers used early in the conflict—simply flew too fast to give the troop carriers sustained support. After one short firing pass against an enemy position, they would have to loop around, often taking more than a minute before they could make a second strike. By then, the troops would already be out of danger, or in serious trouble. But Hueys, jury-rigged with mounts for two .30-caliber machine guns and a pair of rocket pods, could hover above the landing zone and force enemy gunners to keep their heads down while the other helicopters discharged their loads of men. Improvised gun sights—a fancy term for grease-penciled Xs on the canopy bubbles—turned the Hueys into full-fledged gunships. Flying regularly as armed escorts for both Army and Marine assaults, they produced immediate results. Enemy hits on troop-carrying helicopters decreased by fully a third.

Early in 1963 the first factory-equipped gunships arrived in Vietnam. They were Huey Bs, each fitted with four .30-caliber machine guns, a grenade-launcher chin turret mounted under the nose and a pair of three-tube 2.75-inch-rocket pods. The Huey Bs had more powerful engines than the As, but the extra weight and drag of their formidable arsenal (each rocket, for example, weighed 48 pounds) slowed the

Approaching in formation, a Bell assault helicopter unit arrives over an assembly point to pick up American soldiers near the city of Quangngai. The standing GIs holding rifles over their heads mark the spots where the helicopters are to touch down.

gunships so much that they could barely keep up with the venerable Shawnees and Husses they escorted. And as these older transports were replaced with faster Huey troop carriers, called "slicks," the laden gunships, with a top speed of slightly more than 90 miles per hour, were left at a 20-mile-per-hour disadvantage. The slicks—so named because their contours were uncluttered with protruding armament—naturally had to move fast to avoid enemy fire and to achieve surprise, especially since the Huey's innovative semirigid rotor created a reverberating "whap-whap" that could be heard for miles. But to coordinate with their gunship escorts, the slicks were regularly obliged to fly at less than top speed. This problem was not satisfactorily solved until the arrival in 1967 of the first gunship specially designed for the purpose.

The Army recognized the need for such a ship and in 1964 organized a design competition for what it called an Advanced Aerial Fire Support System. Lockheed won the contest in late 1965 with a helicopter called the Cheyenne that promised to have unprecedented speed, maneuverability and firepower. But the Cheyenne was not expected to enter service until the end of the decade, and its complexity and expense caused technical, fiscal and political problems that eventually undermined the project entirely. Meanwhile, the Army opened another competition for an interim gunship. Bell won it with a relatively straightforward extrapolation of the Huey, the Huey Cobra, which was to remain the Army's first-line gunship for more than 15 years.

In essence, the Cobra was a slimmed-down Huey; its fuselage was just 36 inches wide (five feet narrower than the standard Huey) and had room for only a pilot and copilot-gunner sitting one behind the other in a fighter-style cockpit. Its engine was marginally more powerful than that of the earlier Hueys, but it used a new, wide-bladed rotor that gave it a top speed of 219 miles per hour, nearly twice that of a slick. Moreover, the Cobra was far more maneuverable and could carry about three times the armament of earlier gunships—3,000 pounds of rockets, grenades, guns and ammunition—enough in the opinion of some to give it a punch equivalent to that of a jet fighter, since the Cobra, flying right in on top of its target, could put its fire exactly where it was needed.

When the Cobra reached Vietnam in 1967, it had an immediate impact on the War. At last the helicopter could function as a flying weapons platform, as the Army's pioneering helicopter tacticians— Vanderpool's Fools—had envisioned 10 years earlier. Indeed, Cobras were formidable enough to serve as the sole source of firepower when paired with Loaches in two-helicopter teams that would seek out and attack enemy positions. But the Cobra's primary job was, like that of earlier gunships, to give fire support to troop carriers. The difference was that the Cobra could do the job so well that slicks and gunships were able for the first time to work together as true air cavalry.

The first large unit to develop this capability, the 1st Cavalry Division (Airmobile), reached Vietnam two years before the Cobra, but the new gunship, when it arrived, increased the unit's firepower significantly. The 1st had been radically restructured from the outset to achieve airmobility. It was a standard-sized division of 16,000 men, but it had nearly five times the number of helicopters operated by an infantry division; its total of 450 included the Army's first four Skycranes, dozens of Chinooks and scores of Hueys, both slicks and gunships. Its 1,500 ground vehicles—half the number used by an infantry division—were all proportioned for ready transport by helicopter—jeeps, small trucks and backhoes were lifted intact; larger vehicles and equipment in sections that could be quickly reassembled. The division had even given up some of its heavy artillery because it could not be conveniently lifted, though this lack was more than made up for by the presence of airborne firing platforms—rocket-bearing Hueys, and ultimately Cobras.

In a typical air cavalry assault, or "insertion," a brace of Cobras, flying just ahead of the slicks they were escorting, would swoop in over a predetermined landing zone, or LZ as the crews called it, and "hose down" the area with their weapons. The slicks would then fly in and unload their troops as the Cobras hovered alongside, ready to blast away at any enemy gunner who reacted to the landing. The helicopters would hang around only until the LZ had been secured and it was clear that the troops would not need immediate evacuation or fire support.

Many troop insertions encountered little opposition. But from time to time, the enemy was ready and waiting. Early on the morning of March 6, 1969, a routine assault was mounted against an enemy concentration 40 miles north of Saigon. Everything started according to plan: Three

Broad rotor blades and a slim fuselage set the Cobra off from the original Huey, one of which is partially visible on the ground. Pods on the Cobra's stubby wings could carry 52 rockets, and the chin turret, being worked on here by the ground crew, housed a fast-firing machine gun as well as a grenade launcher.

miles from a preselected LZ, two Cobras rendezvoused with a flight of six slicks. At the same time, heavy artillery from a nearby American fire base began to pound the LZ and the dense jungle around it with hundreds of rounds of preparatory fire. One minute before insertion time, a single white-phosphorus shell showered a corner of the LZ with arcing tendrils of brilliant white smoke, signaling to the rapidly approaching helicopters that the artillery barrage was over. Thirty seconds later, the two Cobras dove in to sweep the edges of the LZ with rockets, machine-gun fire and grenades from their chin turrets. Then the six slicks went in, the Cobras flanking them and blasting the edges of the LZ yet again.

The troops jumped clear and moved for the trees as the slicks pulled out, returning to a nearby staging area for a second lift of troops. Someone on the ground radioed, "LZ green"—no enemy fire. The Cobras circled the LZ without firing until the slicks began returning—now one at a time—with the additional troops. Two had already unloaded and a third was about to touch down when the pilots heard on their radios a voice, high-pitched with tension, calling, "The LZ's red, the LZ's red!" It was a trap. Small-arms fire lashed across the clearing, pinning down the newly deposited troops where the helicopters had left them; red tracers floated aloft, reaching out for the two departing slicks and the

A trio of Huey Cobra gunships, each painted with a garish shark's mouth to symbolize their hunter-killer role, cruise above a riverscape in Vietnam.

now furiously attacking gunships. Other voices crowded onto the radio frequency requesting evacuation for a growing number of casualties.

The third slick, hovering just above the LZ, was riddled even before its troops could jump free; the pilot, Warrant Officer David Hughins, pulled pitch, began radioing for help and took his crippled craft back to the staging area. There he and his crew and their troops transferred to another Huey and went back to the LZ. This time he successfully inserted the troops and picked up wounded, but his helicopter was again badly shot up. Back at the staging area, he switched to yet another Huey and picked up a second and then a third load of troops and ammunition. Each time he managed to drop them off and take on more wounded, though he went through a third helicopter in the process. On his last trip, a wounded soldier was shot dead in his door gunner's arms.

By then the ground fire had reached a furious crescendo. Eight more Cobras and four slicks had answered Hughins' call for help, but even with the gunships' suppressive firepower, the American troops were still pinned down. The enemy was well armed, dug-in and spoiling for a fight; the LZ could not be held and the situation was desperate, especially for the wounded. A battalion commander circling low overhead called for a volunteer to pick them up, and the pilot of one of the newly arrived slicks, Warrant Officer Paul Keil, agreed to go in.

As he approached the LZ, a commander on the ground tried to wave him off because the fire was so intense, but Keil went ahead. With a Cobra hovering at each side firing at enemy positions, he landed on the bullet-swept LZ and loaded as many casualties as would fit inside the chopper. He then flew his riddled Huey to a road a few miles away, where he touched down with some of the other slicks. The wounded were transferred from Keil's shot-up wreck to another Huey, and Keil and his crew then jumped into a third, loaded up with ammunition, picked up their Cobra escort and went back in. The fire never slackened. One of the Cobra pilots, Chief Warrant Officer Gary Bishop, reported afterward that Keil "came out of the LZ with bits and pieces coming off the helicopter. He got a copilot wounded; he got a gunner wounded; he got so close the enemy lobbed a hand grenade in and blew the chin bubble completely off the Huey. But he kept coming." On Keil's second trip, his helicopter took 36 hits.

By dusk the last of the wounded had been brought out, and the Cobras had beaten down the ground fire long enough for several Hueys to bring in reinforcements. Bishop and his flight of gunships had refueled and rearmed nine times in the course of the day. The next morning a massive insertion cleared out the ambushing force, but by then the mission of March 6 had already begun to recede in the memories of the participants as one among many, though perhaps worse than most.

Four years and thousands of helicopter missions later, the United States concluded a peace treaty with the North Vietnamese. Even before the signing of the January 1973 cease-fire, U.S. planes had stopped raiding

North Vietnam and the "Vietnamization" of the war in the South had begun, as the South Vietnamese once again took over the fighting. Army helicopter units quickly departed, leaving much of their equipment to the South Vietnamese Air Force, whose men continued the struggle with considerable skill and valor, but against increasing odds.

By July, Marine and Navy helicopter units that had been clearing mines from North Vietnamese waters were gone also. That left, as the total U.S. helicopter presence in all of Southeast Asia, two Air Force squadrons of H-53s stationed in Thailand. They were to evacuate Americans, not from Vietnam, but from Phnom Penh, the capital of Cambodia, if the city seemed about to fall to the antigovernment forces that in five years had all but taken over the country. When Phnom Penh finally did fall in March of 1975, the two Air Force H-53 squadrons were joined by Marine H-53s from the helicopter carrier *Okinawa* in the Gulf of Siam. Operation *Eagle Pull,* the last American military act of the tragic Cambodian War, was executed with sad, smooth precision.

But if the fall of Phnom Penh had long been anticipated, the rapidly ensuing collapse of South Vietnam and the need to evacuate Saigon had not. The Air Force helicopters in Thailand were poorly positioned to reach the South Vietnamese capital; the closest Thai air base was nearly 300 miles from Saigon. And things fell apart so quickly that the Navy and the Marines had not had time to deploy additional carrierborne helicopters into the area. So when, in mid-April, Saigon was about to be overrun, the Air Force helicopters in Thailand flew to the carrier *Midway,* standing off the coast near the city. They, together with the Marine H-53s that had helped evacuate Phnom Penh, and Marine and Navy tandem-rotor CH-46 Sea Knights assigned to ships that happened to be on hand, were to form the core of the evacuation force. A few Hueys belonging to the CIA-funded airline Air America would lend a hand.

When the end came, the helicopters had been standing by for more than a week, and it was clear that they would be the only means of evacuation. Saigon's Tan Son Nhut airfield had been closed down for four days by air attacks carried out by defecting South Vietnamese fighter pilots, and by the threat of enemy artillery. The South Vietnamese forces defending Saigon had been outflanked, and the city lay open for the taking. But U.S. Ambassador Graham Martin, hoping for a cease-fire, delayed activating the frantically pulled together evacuation plan until shortly after noon on April 29. By then it was too late.

The operation should have started with the smooth predawn movement of cars and buses through deserted streets to predesignated collection points, picking up evacuees alerted by telephone and taking them to the U.S. Embassy or the U.S. Defense Attache's Office (DAO) compound at the airport for evacuation. Instead, it began in midafternoon in screaming chaos. Most of the Vietnamese who should have been among the first to go—translators, intelligence analysts, police informants—never reached the collection points; neither did the cars and buses. Many of those who did manage to claw their way into the embas-

A Sikorsky Skycrane lowers cargo containers to besieged Marines at Khe Sanh, near the Laotian border, in 1968. During much of the 77-day siege, helicopters were the only means of supplying the isolated outposts that ringed the main garrison.

sy or DAO compound would have been very low on any rationally ordered list of priority evacuees. Thus, what should have been a methodical dawn-to-dusk grind for the helicopter crews, shuttling back and forth from the evacuation LZs to the receiving ships offshore, became a desperate race against darkness and fatigue.

Their day had started early, with a wake-up by ships' loudspeakers at 2:30 in the morning; by 3:30, the men were in their helicopters, ready to go. But they did not get the Ambassador's call until 1:30 in the afternoon. The craft that did not have auxiliary fuel tanks had to take off, fly to nearby ships to pick up members of a Marine security force who were to ensure that the boarding of evacuees was orderly and then return to their carriers to refuel before picking up evacuees. As a result, the first loads of refugees did not reach the ships until 3:30.

All was confusion. Someone on the DAO staff became concerned about blowing dust on one of the landing areas and had it oiled down. Tracers fired in the chaotic melee that had engulfed the city ignited the fresh oil, and the evacuation force lost three of the 18 pads capable of handling an H-53. The Marines at the DAO compound had only a malfunctioning low-powered radio to communicate with the fleets of incoming helicopters, and someone in downtown Saigon with a far more powerful radio was transmitting incoherently on the same frequency. A couple of hours after dark, with the evacuation still going on, the power in the DAO compound failed, leaving the pads unlighted and the remaining, terrified evacuees huddled in blackened corridors.

The helicopter crews did an extraordinary job under the circumstances. The principal rescue force of Marine, Navy and Air Force helicopters carried more than 7,000 evacuees to safety in that one long day. Volunteer Huey pilots and flight mechanics from Air America braved panicked mobs to shuttle untold numbers of stranded evacuees to the collection points, and then they brought their aircraft out to the ships full. The mere fact that the swarm of helicopters managed to avoid running into one another in the blackness of the tropical night was a fantastic stroke of luck. Finding their way by the light of burning buildings and the lightning flashes of a thunderstorm that stayed clear of the city, the crews continued to work until there were no more evacuees left at their designated pads. That the Marines of the security force in the embassy were not lifted out until the next morning and that 400 would-be evacuees, including some South Korean diplomats and their families, were left behind in the embassy courtyard are not wrongs to be laid at the feet of the air crews. The helicopters and the men who flew them had done all that could have been expected—and then some.

In a concluding note of tragedy, a CH-46 Sea Knight, returning to the carrier *Hancock* from a search-and-rescue mission for downed aviators, attempted to land on the deck but tumbled into the sea and exploded. The two crewmen were rescued, but the pilot and co-pilot died in the crash, the last helicopter casualties of the Vietnam War. ❧

In the final days of the Vietnam War, South Vietnamese Air Force Hueys are jettisoned from the U.S. command ship Blue Ridge to make room for new arrivals during the frantic evacuation of Saigon. Some 6,900 were airlifted by helicopter to waiting American ships stationed in the South China Sea on April 29, 1975.

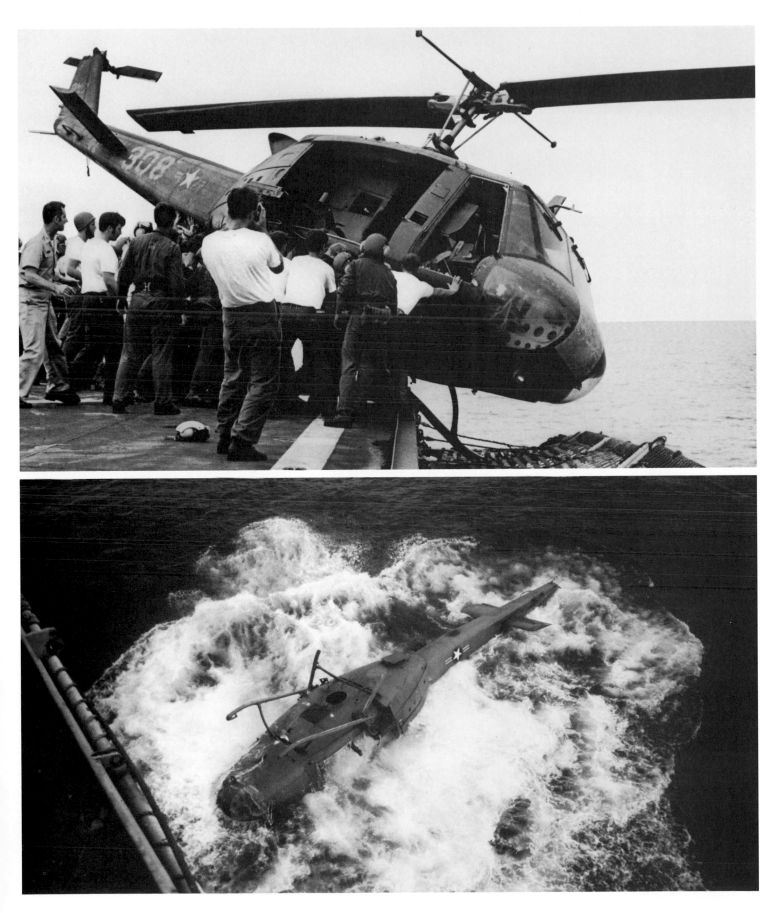

A good and faithful genie

Proved in war, the helicopter has become an efficient and ubiquitous servant of peace, just as Igor Sikorsky envisioned. And as shown on this and the following pages, helicopters play more roles than even that imaginative and humane designer ever dreamed of.

The most dramatic helicopter duty remains the same in peace as in war—rescue. Hovering military and police choppers dangling rescue hoists are literally the life lines for hundreds of victims of catastrophes in inaccessible places—at sea, on remote mountaintops, on the roofs of blazing skyscrapers. And as in Vietnam, helicopters—some of them capable of speeds up to 150 mph—provide the swift transport to medical care that saves the lives of the injured and the ill.

The advantages of a speedy aircraft that can hover, take off and land in the smallest of spaces, and (in some versions) carry loads weighing up to 10 tons have not been lost on farmers and businessmen. Commercial helicopter fleets, many staffed with pilots who served in Vietnam, now serve as couriers for industries that function in remote locations, and as workhorses for activities as diverse as hauling timber, laying pipeline, pouring concrete, dusting crops and herding cattle.

In fact, almost any task that is best done from the air or that requires travel to seemingly unreachable places can be accomplished by helicopter. The machine that Wilbur Wright once thought worthless now proves its worth in every walk of life.

Hovering over a field in East Pakistan—now Bangladesh—a U.S. Army Huey drops food and clothing to survivors of a 1970 cyclone so ravaging that it was called a second Hiroshima. The pilots did not land for fear that starving Pakistanis would be injured by the rotor blades as they surged toward the food.

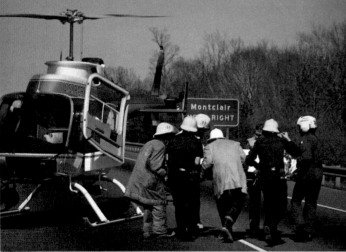

A rescued seaman, dangling beneath an Aérospatiale SA 321 Super Frelon, leaves the sinking supertanker Amoco Cadiz, wrecked off the coast of France in 1978.

U.S. Park Police and firemen rush a badly injured motorist to a helicopter for transport to a hospital shock-trauma unit. Speed saved the 81-year-old victim's life.

His searchlight glowing through curtains of snow, an Air Force pilot hunts for survivors of Air Florida Flight 90, lost in the Potomac River near Washington, D.C., in 1982.

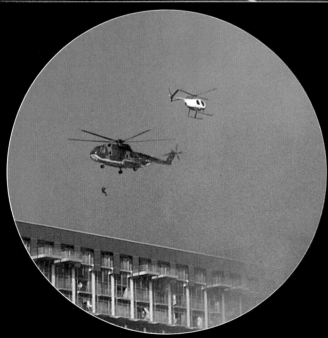

A Sikorsky S-61—one of 11 helicopters involved in the rescue operation—flies a survivor clear of Las Vegas' MGM Grand Hotel during a 1980 fire.

Strapped to a stretcher, the corpse of a luckless mountaineer awaits removal by an Alouette III in the French Alps near Chamonix.

Aided by a rescuer who descended his drifting boat, a bridge worker clings to the hoist of a chopper hovering over Virginia's James Rive

Skyway to anywhere

Personnel and equipment arrive by air at an offshore oil rig far out in the Gulf of Mexico. The trip to the rig takes up to 10 hours by boat, but less than an hour by helicopter.

Too large for all but a few ports, the supertanker Esso Atlantic—shown here off the coast of South Africa—is supplied by helicopters, which can either drop food and mail from the air, or land on the vessel's helipad, which is visible amidships.

A Soviet Mil 4 delivers food and news to ▷ Yakut reindeer herders—shown with their own, simpler form of transportation— in the northeastern reaches of Siberia.

Marvel of agriculture

Sweeping back and forth behind the animals in a swallow's flying pattern, a helicopter drives a herd of cattle across Texas ranchland. Choppers are also used to find and transport strayed or injured cows.

With water scooped up from nearby Lake Arrowhead, a fire department helicopter helps douse blazing brush in Southern California's San Bernardino Mountains.

Plumes of fungicide swirl from a low-flying helicopter as it sprays a German vineyard. The rotor downwash distributes the chemical evenly through the vines.

With its pilot keeping a watchful eye on
events below (inset), a Sikorsky Skycrane
lifts freshly cut timber for transport
from an Oregon logging camp to a mill.
Helicopters eliminate the need to cut
expensive roads to forest logging sites.

With a guiding hand from below, a chopper sets in place a section of pipe—part of a line carrying oil from wells in the Peruvian jungle to the country's west coast. The vapor pattern around the craft is caused by the rotors' disturbance of the hot, humid air.

Hovering high above the choppy water, a Sikorsky Skycrane delivers fresh concrete— the yellow concrete bucket is being steadied by a bridge worker at center—to a segment of the Chesapeake Bay Bridge. The four-mile span, completed in 1973, links Maryland and the Eastern Shore.

In the service of science

A U.S. Geological Survey helicopter deposits two hardy seismographers in the crater of the still-smoking Mount St. Helens. The Washington volcano had erupted only a few weeks previously.

From the door of his low-flying craft, a Montana wildlife officer prepares to toss a capsule of dye—used to trace migration—at the haunch of a fleeing young moose.

Caught and netted by a cowboy, a Grand
Canyon burro—its appetite and destructive
hooves a menace to canyon ecology—
gets a chopper ride to a new home.

Airborne supplies reach a scientists' camp
high on Antarctica's Byrd Glacier. Crevasses
make the ice almost impassable.

Tranquilized and neatly trussed up in a
net, an Alaskan polar bear is hoisted by
helicopter and weighed by a U.S. Fish
and Wildlife survey team.

For fun, profit and patrol

Arriving passengers at New York's La Guardia Airport head for a six-minute helicopter ride to downtown Manhattan.

Traveling businessmen hold a time-saving conference in flight. Helicopter transportation is useful for large corporations with branch offices and plants difficult to reach by conventional aircraft.

Deposited by helicopter on usually
inaccessible slopes high in British
Columbia's Bugaboo mountain range,
four lucky skiers start a spectacular,
miles-long run over virgin snow.

Sailing over a busy Los Angeles freeway,
a California Highway patrolman monitors
the flow of traffic. Police helicopters
also are used for locating accidents—
and for setting speed traps.

Acknowledgments

The index for this book was prepared by Gale Linck Partoyan. The editors also wish to thank: **In Denmark:** Copenhagen—Inge Thier, Foreign Ministry. **In France:** Demmarie-lès-Lys—Maurice Claisse; Paris—Odile Benoist, Yvan Kayser, Général Pierre Lissarague, Director, Général Roger de Ruffray, Deputy Director, Colonel Pierre Willefert, Curator, Musée de l'Air; Vincennes—Marcellin Hodeir, S.H.A.A. **In Great Britain:** London—John Hewish, British Library; E. C. Hine, Alan Williams, Imperial War Museum; Arnold Nayler, Royal Aeronautical Society; Andrew Cormack, Peter Merton, Royal Air Force Museum; John Bagley, Martin Andrewartha, Science Museum; Marjorie Willis, BBC Hulton Picture Library; Surrey—Philip

Jarratt. **In Italy:** Milan—Fabrizio Bovi, Agusta; Alfredo Hummel, Publifoto Notizie; Maurizio Pagliano; Rome—Nino Arena; Countess Maria Fede Caproni, Museo Aeronautico Caproni di Taliedo; Cesare Falessi, Aeritalia. **In Spain:** Madrid—José Warleta Carrillo. **In the United States:** Alabama—Harry R. Fletcher, Maxwell Air Force Base; California—Peter G. Dorland, Fort Irwin; Connecticut—Malcolm Burgess, Linda Evans, Maureen Marren, Dorothy Morris, Sergei Sikorsky, Sikorsky Aircraft Company; Washington, D.C.—Brigadier General Robert F. Molinelli, the Pentagon; Albert E. Crowdrey, William J. Webb, U.S. Army Center of Military History; Earl Cronin, Dennis Doyle, Donald Usher, Aviation Section, U.S.

Park Police; Stuart S. Roberts, M.D., St. Francis Hospital; Maryland—John M. Slattery; New York—Carter Harman, Composers Recordings, Inc.; Pennsylvania—Frank Kauffman, Boeing Vertol, Inc.; Texas—Rudeford M. Norman, Fort Hood; Martin C. Reisch, Bell Helicopter; Virginia—Bob Brownell; Colonel Emmett F. Knight, Fort Eustis. **In West Germany:** Babenhausen—Heinz Nowarra; Bückeburg—Werner Nöltemeyer, Hubschrauber Museum; Koblenz—Meinrad Nilges, Bundesarchiv; Munich—Kyrill von Gersdorff, Deutsches Museum; West Berlin—Dr. Roland Klemig, Heidi Klein, Bildarchiv Preussischer Kulturbesitz; Wolfgang Streubel, Ullstein Bilderdienst.

Bibliography

Books
Becker, Beril, *Dreams and Realities of the Conquest of the Skies.* Atheneum, 1968.
Brown, Joseph Mill, *Helicopter Directory.* David & Charles Ltd., 1976.
Chanute, Octave, *Progress in Flying Machines.* Lorenz & Herweg, 1976.
Collier, Basil, *A History of Air Power.* Macmillan, 1974.
De La Cierva, Juan, and Don Rose, *Wings of Tomorrow: The Story of the Autogiro.* Brewer, Warren & Putnam, 1931.
Delear, Frank J.:
Helicopters and Airplanes of the U.S. Army. Dodd, Mead & Company, 1977.
Igor Sikorsky: His Three Careers in Aviation. Dodd, Mead & Company, 1976.
Dollfus, Charles, *Histoire de L'Aéronautique.* Paris, 1942.
Drendel, Lou, *Gunslingers in Action.* Squadron/Signal Publications, 1974.
Fails, William R., *Marines and Helicopters, 1962-1973.* U.S. Marine Corps, 1978.
Francis, Devon, *The Story of the Helicopter.* Coward-McCann, Inc., 1946.
Gablehouse, Charles, *Helicopters and Autogiros: A Chronicle of Rotating-wing Aircraft.* J. B. Lippincott, 1967.

Gessow, Alfred, and Garry C. Myers Jr., *Aerodynamics of the Helicopter.* Frederick Ungar, 1952.
Gibbs-Smith, Charles Harvard:
Aviation: An Historical Survey from its Origins to the end of World War II. London: Her Majesty's Stationery Office, 1970.
The Inventions of Leonardo Da Vinci. Charles Scribner's Sons, 1978.
Gregory, Hollingsworth Franklin, *The Helicopter.* A. S. Barnes and Company, 1976.
Gunston, Bill, and John Batchelor, *Helicopters at War.* Chartwell Books Inc., 1977.
Hubler, Richard G., *Straight Up: The Story of Vertical Flight.* Duell, Sloan and Pearce, 1961.
Lambermont, Paul, and Anthony Pirie, *Helicopters and Autogyros of the World/Revised Edition.* A. S. Barnes and Company, 1970.
Liptrot, R. N., and J. D. Woods, *Rotorcraft.* London: Butterworths Scientific Publications, 1955.
Michelet, Guy, *Breguet.* Paris: Éditions France—Empire, 1963.
Morris, Charles Lester, *Pioneering the Helicopter.* McGraw-Hill, 1945.
Munson, Kenneth, *Helicopters and other Rotorcraft since 1907.* Macmillan, 1968.

Rawlins, Eugene W., *Marines and Helicopters, 1946-1962.* U.S. Marine Corps, 1976.
Sikorsky, Igor I., *The Story of the Winged-S: Late Developments and Recent Photographs of the Helicopter.* Dodd, Mead & Company, 1967.
Taylor, John W. R., *Helicopters and VTOL Aircraft.* Doubleday, 1960.
Taylor, John W. R., and Kenneth Munson, *History of Aviation.* Crown, 1972.
Taylor, Michael J. H., and John W. R. Taylor, *Helicopters of the World.* Charles Scribner's Sons, 1978.

Periodicals
Focke, Henrich, "German Thinking on Rotary-wing Development." *Journal of the Royal Aeronautical Society,* May 1965.
Foltmann, John, "A Visionary Proved Right." *Danish Foreign Office Journal,* May 1956.
Grosz, Peter, "Helicopter Pioneers of World War I." *Air Enthusiast,* March-June 1978.
Gunther, Carl R., "Autogiro: The World's First Commercially Successful Rotary-wing Aircraft." *Popular Rotorcraft Flying,* October-December 1979.
Liptrot, R. N., "Historical Development of Helicopters." *American Helicopter,* March 1947.

Picture credits

Sources for the illustrations in this book are shown below. Credits from left to right are separated by semicolons, from top to bottom by dashes. Endpaper (and cover detail, regular edition): Painting by John Young. 6, 7: Danish Ministry for Foreign Affairs, Copenhagen. 8, 9: National Archives, No. 18-WP-16783. 10, 11: S.H.A.A., Vincennes, France. 12, 13: Courtesy Sikorsky Aircraft. 14, 15: Courtesy Musée de l'Air, Le Bourget, France. 16: Library of Congress. 18: Royal Library, Copenhagen. 19: Photo Bulloz, courtesy Bibliothèque de l'Institut de France, Paris. 21: The British Library, Science Reference Library, London. 22: National Air and Space Museum, Smithsonian Institution, No. A4249A—Museo Aeronautico Caproni di Taliedo, Rome. 23: Ullstein Bilderdienst, Berlin (West)—Bildar-

chiv Preussischer Kulturbesitz, Berlin (West)—Ullstein Bilderdienst, Berlin (West). 26: Courtesy the Connecticut Aeronautical Historical Association. 28, 29: S.H.A.A., Vincennes, France, inset, Collection Viollet, Paris. 31: Musée de l'Air, Le Bourget, France. 32: Courtesy Jean Devaux, Paris. 34, 35: Courtesy United Technologies Corporation. 37: The Science Museum, London. 38, 39: The Kansas State Historical Society, Topeka; Collection Viollet, Paris. 40: Chicago Historical Society DN No. L8653—Brown Brothers. 42-47: Edison National Historical Site, National Park Service, U.S. Department of Interior. 48, 49: National Air and Space Museum, Smithsonian Institution, No. 79-6690; National Archives No. 18-WP-17716. 50: Mary Evans Picture Library, London. 53-55: Artwork by Another Color, Inc.

57: Robert Royal, courtesy of the De la Cierva family, Madrid. 58: BBC Hulton Picture Library, London. 59, 61: Robert Royal, courtesy of the De la Cierva family, Madrid. 62, 63: Derek Bayes, courtesy the Royal Air Force Museum, Hendon. 64, 65: National Air and Space Museum, Smithsonian Institution, No. 82-5392. 66: Museo Aeronautico Caproni di Taliedo, Rome. 67: National Air and Space Musum, Smithsonian Institution, No. 82-5390. 68: Courtesy United Technologies Corporation. 70: Painting by Achille Beltrame, courtesy Domenica del Corriere, Milan. 72: Musée de l'Air, Le Bourget, France. 74: Süddeutscher Verlag Bilderdienst, Munich—Ullstein Bilderdienst, Berlin (West). 75: VFW, Bremen. 76: Courtesy Heinz J. Nowarra, Babenhausen, Federal Republic of Germany. 77: Courtesy Unit-

Index